BEGGARS OR ANGELS

How a Single Mother Triumphed Over War, Welfare
and Cancer to Become a Successful Philanthropist

ROSEMARY TRAN LAUER
Founder, Devotion to Children

WITH SCOTT BELLER

Some names and identifying details of people described in this book have been changed or omitted to protect their privacy.

© 2013 Rosemary Tran Lauer
Published by DTC Press, LLC
All Rights Reserved

No part of this book may be reproduced in any form or by any means, electronic or mechanical, including photocopying, recording or by any information storage and retrieval system, without permission in writing from DTC Press, LLC.

DTC Press, LLC
2979 Westhurst Lane, Oakton, VA 22124
http://dtcpress.com

ISBN 978-0-9863219-0-0
Third edition: January 2015

Cover photo and design by Roberto Nickson. Edited by Taylor Mallory Holland. Interior design and page layout by Scott Beller.

Rosemary Tran Lauer

*My thanks to God for Bill, my children & the
children of the world—I love you*

Scott Beller

*For Elisabeth, Morgan & Lauren,
my reasons "why"*

"The central struggle of parenthood is to let our hopes for our children outweigh our fears."

Ellen Goodman

"Those who are not looking for happiness are the most likely to find it, because those who are searching forget that the surest way to be happy is to seek happiness for others."

Martin Luther King, Jr.

Giấc mộng tīm nhau tīm chẳng thấy
Mênh mang biển hận, hận không bờ
Trời thu ảm đạm một mầu
Gió thu hiu hắt thêm rầu lõng em

Vainly searching for each other in dreams,
We found only immense shoreless sorrow.
In autumn sky painted a mournful hue,
Its gentle wind saddens my heart.

Opening lines of "Giot Le Thu" ("Autumn Tears"), 1923,
by my grandmother Tüöng Phố
Translated August 18, 2009, by Thomas D. Le

Contents

Introduction: Keeping a Promise — 1

PART I: VIETNAM

Chapter 1	Everything Happens for a Reason	7
Chapter 2	Calm before the Storm	17
Chapter 3	War and Women	29
Chapter 4	Sink or Swim	41
Chapter 5	Adrift	53

PART II: AMERICA

Chapter 6	From One Boogeyman to Another	69
Chapter 7	Running to Stand Still	81
Chapter 8	Flight of the Bumblebee	93
Chapter 9	Lather, Rinse, Repeat	113
Chapter 10	Roots of Devotion	131
Chapter 11	Long Way Home	151

PART III: TRANSFORMATION

Chapter 12	Anguish, Beauty and Bliss	167
Chapter 13	Rejuvenation	191
Chapter 14	Transformed and Ascending	219

Epilogue: A Legacy ... for Other People's Children — 223

BEGGARS OR ANGELS

Introduction: *Keeping a Promise*

I was born in South Vietnam, a nation impoverished by centuries of invasion, conflict and oppression. My family was not poor, nor were we rich. In the U.S., we might have been considered "middle class." Though I was not yet aware of it growing up, I was very lucky. Many other Vietnamese children weren't as fortunate. Their harsh reality, thrust upon them through no fault of their own, has weighed on my heart and mind for as long as I can remember.

When I was nine years old, I went with my older brother Minh to visit a local orphanage. The building, a supposed refuge for deprived and abandoned children, was an oversized, third-world hovel. Sad though it was, this was the best a few dedicated nuns could provide and it was better than the lonesome streets, where many children lived without shelter, food or anyone to care for them.

I remember wading into a crowd of toddlers—all eager to play, laugh and eat. Mostly, they just wanted someone to pay attention to them. But there weren't enough nuns to take care of so many children and, though I'm sure they tried their very best to tend to each and every child, it must have been an impossible task, given their lack of resources.

When it was time to go, I didn't want to leave. I longed to take them all home with me and love them the way they deserved. What I took with me, instead, was the glimmer of hope I saw in their eyes as they looked back at me, smiling and probably thinking that maybe, just maybe, this would be the day they would finally get to go home. I left the orphanage with a sense of hopelessness. But I told myself that someday, when I was older, I would do something to help those children and others like them.

From an early age, I had very strong motherly instincts and loved children. As a kid, when I played house with my brothers and sisters, I always wanted to be the mother, helping to raise happy kids. Perhaps part of me simply wanted to show the world that one person who cares could make a real difference in the lives of others.

After escaping the war in Vietnam with my two young children, I battled adversity in America for decades. Maybe it was supposed to take that long for me to gain the strength, faith and perspective I needed to understand my life's purpose and to finally learn the meaning of true love. Not surprisingly, I've found the concepts to be closely linked. If you find one, you're sure to find the other. My true loves are my children and my current husband Bill. And my purpose is Devotion to Children, the philanthropic organization I founded in 1994.

My life has been a good one, but it's also been filled with struggles. Over the years, I've adopted the motto "everything happens for a reason"—a philosophy that rang as true for me as a Buddhist in my early days in Vietnam as it has for me as a converted Christian here in the U.S. This simple phrase has comforted me through war, two unconventional divorces, poverty, homelessness and even cancer. As you continue reading my story, you'll travel with me along my turbulent journey from being a young Vietnamese girl, to a dutiful homemaker, a desperate and homeless single mother, to the passionate American philanthropist I am today.

It's now clear to me that Devotion to Children is one of the ultimate reasons "why" everything has happened the way it has in my life. In coming to terms with my own experiences, I've chosen to live the years I have left doing all I can to help those in need: families with young children in challenging situations, women, single mothers and fathers, other immigrants and small business owners. In short, people who have found themselves alone, physically or emotionally, while trying to navigate extreme, unfamiliar circumstances with no direction and no safety net. No "normal." Having been there myself, I want to help make their journeys a little less difficult.

According to the Childhood Poverty Research and Policy Center, an estimated 600 million children today live in poverty worldwide. That is about one in four. Even in the U.S., nearly one in five children is poor, according to a 2010 study by the Urban Institute. And roughly half of them will be persistently poor. In other words, they'll live in poverty for at least half their childhoods.

During these harsh economic times, with ongoing debates over social services and immigration issues, millions of families in the U.S. are still looking for ways to make ends meet. I want to encourage them not to give up, not to blame themselves or resort to extreme measures to survive. With faith, effort, the right choices, a dash of grace and some luck thrown in for good measure, we all can give our children and ourselves what we deserve: a peaceful, healthy, fulfilling existence.

Although war was the main reason my children and I left our home country and their father behind, my story—and this book—is not about war and its many horrors. In fact, my life in Vietnam is only the prelude to an even greater adventure that began when I took my first hesitant steps aboard a westward-bound ship in the Port of Saigon. Those small steps launched a fight for survival, a quest to understand my personal reasons "why," and a mission to let other children and families know there is always hope and they are never alone.

PART I

VIETNAM

Chapter 1: *Everything Happens for a Reason*

Growing up in Vietnam, I knew exactly what was expected of me. In the Asian culture, it's believed the ideal life for a woman is to grow up proper, get married, raise children and then live happily ever after. And that's just what I planned to do. I didn't know that such fairytales are routinely interrupted by the conflicts, heartbreaks and unexpected detours of real life. I know this now.

Because I was raised in a Buddhist culture, I was taught to believe that people who lead challenged lives or fall upon hard times must have negative karma. In other words, bad things happen for a reason, and the reason is that you must have done something wrong in a past life. I've never been able to accept this philosophy. Two lifetimes of experience have taught me differently.

To be clear, I'm not talking about reincarnation. The first lifetime that changed how I see the world was not my own; it was my grandmother's.

My grandmother, Tüöng Phố, was beloved throughout Vietnam for her poetry. Her poems invoked breathtaking imagery to express the most profound, heartrending and romantic sentiments. In her art and in her life, she embodied the avant-garde. And in the oppressive Vietnamese society of the early 20th century, she courageously followed her own path.

She married my grandfather when she was quite young and was soon with child. While she was pregnant, my grandfather was called away to practice medicine in France. But after several months abroad, he fell ill with tuberculosis and returned home to his family. A few months later, my grandfather passed away—leaving my grandmother alone with her son.

As a way to express and perhaps release some of the paralyzing anguish of losing her husband of only two years, my grandmother wrote

Autumn Tears in 1923. She was a teacher at the time and not yet a full-time poet. This work brought her almost instant recognition throughout Vietnam. She was young, beautiful and suddenly famous.

In that time and culture, however, peering public eyes coldly chose to focus on something else: she was now a single mother. The situation didn't sit well with people. Even though my grandmother was a widow, many of those in her community believed a "good" woman with children must have a husband in order to maintain her honor and dignity. So her parents quickly arranged for her to wed a man who was wealthy, powerful and extremely influential in the local community.

Money and status didn't matter to my grandmother, but her will to resist was weakened by her grief and love for my grandfather. She gave into societal pressure and her parents' wishes. She remarried to appease them all, but she never again allowed herself to love another man.

If not for her son, my grandmother might have given up on the life she now considered broken and out of her control. My father became her will to live, and her poetry became her escape. Together, her child and creative writing nourished her. In him she found renewed reason to strive for a fulfilling life, while her painful circumstances provided unlimited fuel for her poems. Each and every line she wrote radiated with sorrow.

Just after I was born, my grandmother read my star chart, which revealed to her that my life would also be complicated. To Buddhists, "complicated" is often synonymous with "hardships"—which means bad karma, something for which many believe there can be no forgiveness. My grandmother worried I might someday endure a life as difficult as hers, maybe worse. To change my destiny, she suggested to my parents that I pursue ordination as a Buddhist nun, even though doing so would divert me from the ideal married-with-children, happily-ever-after Vietnamese experience.

I didn't become a nun. And despite my life's many twists and turns and highs and lows, I still believe my decision was the right one for me.

Although I never made it to the safety of a monastery, my grandmother was always there to serve as my guardian. I was the seventh of fourteen children and even lower in the pecking order because I was small. I became tough out of necessity. My older and younger brothers routinely beat me up and called it "playing." They also told me, "You're ugly, and nobody will ever want to marry you. You'll be an old maid!" Rough as they were, I considered their abuse the price of being included.

My grandmother gave me refuge from my brothers. I don't know why she seemed to favor me over my siblings. Maybe because of my unsettling star chart, she felt we shared a deeper connection than she had with any of her other grandchildren. Whatever her reasons and no matter how strict she could be, I always took solace in knowing my grandmother deemed herself my protector from the very beginning.

She was also my first teacher. I was just three years old when she began drilling me daily on my multiplication tables. This was not shocking because I was a toddler, but because I was a girl. Within that repressed society, it mattered more that Vietnamese girls be able to cook, embroider, display good manners and please people than it did for them to get an education. And above all, it mattered whether they were pretty enough to marry rich. But my grandmother was different, so she insisted I be different too. She wanted more for me—and expected more from me—than to be just another pretty object, ready and willing to serve a wealthy husband. She wanted me to shine from the inside out.

So I joined my grandmother each day in her tiny, tin-roofed kitchen. The little hut, screened in with bamboo and situated across from the main house, was her private "workshop." While she sat hunched over on her stool, tending clay pots bubbling on two coal-burning stoves, I would sit in the corner, practicing my math skills. And I would sweat. My seemingly endless recitations of "two by two equals four ... two by three equals six ..." and so on cut through 100-degree air thick with humidity and the sugary, sharp aroma of *omai,* her famed candied plum and pickle treats. If I said them all correctly, I got to eat. Those treats were a great incentive for me to become a quick study and a constant threat to spoil my concentration ... and my dinner!

On the hottest days, when it seemed my brain was searing faster than the food on my grandmother's stove, her rigorous teaching methods and attention didn't feel very loving. They felt more like punishment. I didn't yet understand that as she prepared her heavenly confections, she was also preparing me to appreciate the value of an education and instilling in me a lifelong hunger for knowledge.

Despite my efforts to obtain one, I never actually received a college degree. Instead I earned a diploma from cosmetology school. When I remember the way my grandmother disapproved of me wearing too much makeup as a teenager, I can't help but smile. Pointing at my painted eyes, she would say, "Little one, you don't need all that." The funny thing is that without "all that," I might not have made it very far in America.

For that journey, one I would not make until many years later, I did not need my grandmother's math lessons. But I did need her courage, strength and independent spirit ... and a whole lot of faith.

My earliest memories of exposure to religion are filled with wild tales of horror. In Nha Trang, where I grew up, there lurked what may best be described as a mobile museum of torture. For a few pennies, kids could tour a dozen, graphic scenes of hell—from which we learned such vital lessons as "if you lie, the devil will cut your tongue out," "look at bad things and he'll poke out your eyes," "steal and he'll cut your hands off" and "if you don't finish your food, you'll go to hell, and the food will turn to maggots in your mouth." The torture truck stalked amusement parks, playgrounds, and a variety of other places impressionable children went for fun.

There was also a Catholic church in town, built by the French. People always tried to scare me away from it. When I was four years old, my friends told me not to go near "that place." They could not bring themselves to actually call it a church. Misled about the details of the Eucharist, they warned, "They capture kids in there. They'll kill you, then drink your blood and grind up your bones to make bread!" It was an interesting interpretation of "eat/drink this in remembrance of Me."

Thankfully, my exploration of religion and faith became much more substantive and informed as I matured. Even as I was immersed in a Buddhist culture, my curiosity (inherited from my grandmother) and my need for more spiritual completeness pushed me towards Catholicism.

I was fourteen or fifteen years old, living in Da Lat, when curiosity finally got the best of me. Feeling adventurous, I crept inside the back door of the town's largest Catholic church to see what all the controversy was about. I found a safe spot to sit—back row, near the entrance, on the aisle—to ensure myself a quick getaway at the first sign of danger... or blood.

It was a weekday afternoon. Candles glowed along the nave and near the altar in what was otherwise a darkened sanctuary, creating a warm, welcoming environment. I scanned the darkness to take in as much detail as I could. The shadowy place was less than half full. Scattered throughout the rows of pews were a handful of parishioners—mostly older women who'd come to pray in silence.

My eyes were eventually drawn to a tall, thin, very naked man on display. Mounted to a wooden cross at the front of the church, he wore nothing but a crown of thorns. Mimicking what I saw others doing, I knelt in the dark for half an hour, staring at Him. I had no idea who he was or what he had done to deserve such a fate.

Looking up at the altar, I suddenly noticed a halo of light around the slim figure. Though dim at first, the shimmering halo slowly grew brighter until it beamed like a flare. I thought it must be some kind of trick, like in the movies, but quickly dismissed the idea of something so crazy happening in a church in Da Lat. The brilliant light, I realized, must be some kind of sign that I was in the right place. It was beautiful.

When I left that day, I was excited and more than a little relieved I had survived my first visit to a Catholic church. I longed to go back. I needed to learn more.

While still attending the Buddhist Temple for traditional Vietnamese ceremonies, I began attending mass regularly—usually as an observer and outsider. Once in a while, I went with my mother, who was also looking for new spiritual fulfillment.

On Sundays, crowds overflowed onto the street. I often had to stand outside with hundreds of others, even in the cold of winter. Sometimes I listened to the sermons; other times I didn't. Just to be near the activity and energy of the church and its parishioners invigorated me. I knew nothing about Christianity, but that didn't matter. It was satisfying enough just to feel connected to something greater than myself. It felt right.

As I got older, my faith steadily progressed from its Buddhist roots to Catholicism and finally, to the broader study of Christianity. Buddhism taught me many valuable lessons that I still live by. It showed me that while introspection and inner peace are important, one must also develop love and compassion for others. This philosophy is the basis for my belief that you can't give to others something you don't already have—whether it's wisdom, kindness, love or money.

However, Buddhism also constantly reminded me about negative karma—a concept that troubled me. I didn't know whether I had any past lives, and I could not remember doing anything particularly bad as a child. So why should I take the blame or pay for something I had no memory of doing?

While Buddhism preached bad karma, Christianity promised forgiveness. The more I learned about Christianity, the more I embraced it. I didn't believe that people should be slaves to their pasts—and certainly not to past lives. By overcoming hardship and leaving the past behind, anybody could turn struggle into something positive. Meaning could emerge from chaos. Glory from suffering. This perspective was hopeful, inspirational and empowering.

Throughout my spiritual transformation, I came to believe that faith in God, freewill and determination could provide the strength to conquer anything. And I was going to need that strength, because life would get difficult quickly.

The first time I met an American woman was on a spring day in 1974. I was twenty-one years old, the mother of a young son, still practically a newlywed, and blissfully ignorant of the dangerous situation brewing close to my home.

I awoke to a glimmering sun and a light breeze whispering through my bedroom window. The air was warmer than usual and gave no hint of the civil war ravaging Vietnam. In that moment, I didn't have reason to think I would need to evacuate my home in Pleiku just a year later. For the time being, my world was beautifully serene.

Binh, my husband of three years, was already dressed and ready for work. I was reluctant, as always, to leave the comfort of our bed. There was something about lingering beneath cotton-stuffed blankets that gave me an added sense of calm and security.

Before heading to his office, Binh came into our room and asked, "Do you want to go on a field trip with me to Kon Tum?" As an intelligence officer stationed in Pleiku—a key base for the South Vietnamese and U.S. armies—my husband frequently served as a local guide to the Central Highland region for allied personnel and other Western visitors. That day he was to host a small group on a tour of Kon Tum, which was about fifty miles north.

Remote and mountainous, Kon Tum could never hope to be as popular with tourists as Da Lat or Saigon. But Binh told me there were bountiful *vu sua* (star apple) orchards there. Excited by this exotic delicacy and the opportunity to go someplace new, I jumped from bed and promised to be ready in an hour.

When we arrived at his headquarters, Binh and I climbed into another Jeep with three people who had just arrived from Saigon. I was surprised to see that two of them were Americans—a Caucasian man and woman. I didn't know why they'd come to Vietnam or why they were interested in our local produce. I was much more interested in exploring Kon Tum's wilderness and the promise of its fragrant fruit trees.

On the ride north, I learned that the man, whose name was Fox, was a writer for *The New York Times*. The woman was his girlfriend. With them was a Vietnamese photographer. This information about their business in Vietnam raised my curiosity slightly.

Kon Tum province is the northernmost region of Vietnam's Central Highlands. The area had been the site of significant fighting during past wars. Even today, there are many decaying weapons and artillery shells scattered throughout the territory. That these American journalists were headed to Kon Tum should have signaled to me that conflict was again headed towards the region—and soon to my very doorstep. But rather than consider what seemed like such an unlikely possibility, I again surrendered myself to the more pleasurable thought of harvesting sweet *vu sua*.

On our return trip, with my appetite for adventure and star apples sated, I finally turned my attention to our traveling companions, particularly the woman. I had immediately noticed her beauty and that she was much taller than I was. Studying her now, I also noted her delicately-sculpted nose and the big green eyes framed beneath glittering crescents of eye shadow.

I tried to ask what kind of makeup she used, but she didn't understand my attempts to communicate. Using a combination of limited English, simple Vietnamese and hand gestures, I finally got my point across. With smiling eyes, she pulled a compact out of her bag and proceeded to share one of her beauty secrets.

The trip was fruitful in more ways than one. I would not realize until years later, when I was far from Kon Tum and my homeland, that these two Americans were among the many angels who would change the course of my life—her by sparking my interest in cosmetology and him by helping me as I tried, in the midst of great chaos, to find a way out of Vietnam for my children and myself.

Chapter 2: *Calm before the Storm*

Rarely did I encounter Americans in my daily life in Pleiku, but when I did, they were usually soldiers. For a "proper" Vietnamese woman, associating with Americans for any reason was frowned upon. If spotted alone in the company of a "Caucasian devil," you were assumed to be providing "special services" for quick money. Aside from those who came into the PX to get film developed while I worked there one summer, I had almost no interaction with American G.I.s or civilians. I mostly saw them from a distance. They were a curiosity—like movie stars from Hollywood. I didn't understand much about their culture or language and assumed they didn't understand mine either. What I knew about Americans I learned from gossip passed along by family and friends.

Most South Vietnamese citizens regarded the U.S. forces as just another group of oppressors, not as liberators. Many believed Americans brought widespread destruction to the region and spurred an increase in prostitution and other vices. Americans were either celebrities or dark, imposing figures—invaders with the notorious reputation for helping to further corruption in a country. These are the things I thought I knew about Americans before I really got to know Fox, the reporter from *The New York Times*.

One late spring afternoon in 1974, a few months after our trip to Kon Tum, Fox showed up at our door. Binh was in Saigon for work, so I was home alone and very pregnant with my second child, our daughter, Mai.

Although I immediately recognized Fox, I was confused about why he had come to our house. My husband always held business meetings at his office on base, not at home. I attempted a few words in English to apologize for his having made an unnecessary trip, explaining that Binh was away on TDY (or "temporary duty yonder," military speak for out of town) and that I was not sure when he would return.

Fox seemed disappointed. His eyes darted about, as if searching for another reason to stay. He said he had other business but would return later that evening so we could go to eat. This confused me even more. Maybe he had not understood me when I said Binh was away and would be gone for several days. I tried at first to decline his invitation but finally relented. Something about the soft-spoken, intellectual American journalist interested me—something in his awkward, yet sincere, manner.

As promised, Fox returned a few hours later. I chose a restaurant within walking distance to avoid taking a *cyclo,* or bicycle taxi, which was a common mode of transportation in Pleiku. Unless riding with her husband or a male relative, a proper lady knew not to share a *cyclo* with a man. And though well-camouflaged beneath my stylish pink maternity dress with an empire waist and halter top, my protruding belly would have made contact unavoidable in one of the tiny *cyclos.* Any physical contact with a man—a strange Caucasian, at that—would have been scandalous. So we walked, Fox in his rumpled business suit and me in my finest maternity wear.

The restaurant, a popular Chinese place, was no bigger than most American gourmet kitchens and had only three or four small tables in the entire dining room. It was a slow night for business, and our table was one of just two that were occupied. Hints of light flickered from candle stubs in votives sprinkled around the room, not for ambiance, but because the proprietors could not afford electricity. The dim lighting also helped conceal the filth surrounding the patrons. Health inspectors from a Western nation might have shut down the dingy hole-in-the-wall long before. Regardless, this was considered a fine-dining experience for the residents living in Pleiku at the time.

Though we had walked to the restaurant in silence, once wedged into our seats, we began to attempt simple conversation. My contribution to our small talk consisted of a few words in French and even fewer in English; all were tied loosely together by hand gestures. Sitting in public, pregnant, with an American I barely knew and could scarcely understand was one of the more uncomfortable moments of my life. But the more I talked to him, the more Fox put me at ease.

He struck me as a thoughtful introvert—calm, curious and polite. He had the look of a proper gentleman, not because of his clothes, but because of the way he carried himself. He was not a strikingly handsome man, but his overall pleasant appearance made him attractive. Easily ten to fifteen years my senior, he didn't have much hair, but what he had was well groomed, and I thought this added to his distinguished look. He had a sophistication that came naturally, as though he never had to try hard to achieve it.

Despite the fact I could not understand much of what Fox said, I was eager to learn more about him and all the worldly things he knew. For these and other reasons I can't quite express, Fox impressed me as a person of good character—someone I could trust.

After listening to Fox talk a while about his work and where he was from, I tried to tell him about my family. I wanted to reassure him that, despite the humble restaurant to which I had brought him, I came from an honorable Vietnamese family, one descended from nobility. With raised eyebrows, he said, "Oh, so you mean you're a snob?"

The word "snob" was unfamiliar to me in any language. It sounded a little like the French word noblesse, which means "nobility." Because he was smiling, I assumed he understood me. Had I been more sensitive to the nuances of English, I might have realized he was teasing me and become upset. Instead, I returned his smile and meekly responded with one of the few phrases I knew well, "Yes, thank you."

The rest of our conversation was punctuated with similar awkwardness and mistranslations. Thankfully, he was a very patient man. As a journalist, he was probably used to dealing with people who would not—or, as in my case, could not—tell him what he wanted to know.

At first, I thought our mutual attraction was due to natural curiosity.

But in the nearly forty years since our dinner in Pleiku, I've realized ours was a more complex connection—a genuine admiration and a sense of familiarity uncommon for two people who barely knew each other.

Our connection had begun during our walk through Kon Tum months earlier with my husband and Fox's tour group. Fox and his battlefield photographer probably were there to unearth stories buried beneath the surface of war and reveal the plight of the Vietnamese people to the world. As we wandered among the exotic bamboo and *vu sua* trees, I remember asking, "Can you take my picture?" I was excited to be there and thought a human subject might help make their photos livelier. They may have intended to convey the harsh reality of war, but there I was, all innocence and smiles, dancing against the backdrop of a once-and-future battlefield. I was the naïve girl in that old saying, "What's a nice girl like you doing in a place like this?"

Now, in Pleiku, I was once again a vivacious, well-dressed, well-mascara'd young woman looking content in the middle of a war-threatened setting. To see me thriving in this environment—maybe in spite of it—seemed to impress Fox. Maybe he wanted to help me. Maybe he thought someone should take me away from all this. Whatever the reason, we were drawn together despite our many differences. That awkward night, regardless of our language barrier, I felt we understood one another. Fox and I developed an unusual relationship. It took many years for me to understand the reason our lives had crossed paths.

When we returned to my house, Fox handed me a slip of paper with his contact information in Saigon and then left without a word. Exchanging personal information may have been normal for Americans—as natural as new acquaintances trading business cards. But in Vietnam, such sharing was an intimate act and uncommon between strangers. The weight of this gesture was undeniable, even if I could not define it. Maybe Fox knew something I didn't about the war's progress. Pleiku was close to the frontlines, and as a war correspondent who had traveled throughout the country and seen how far the fighting had spread, maybe Fox knew my family and I could be in danger soon. Maybe he was letting me know he would help if I ever needed it. But at the time, there was no reason to think we would need to leave Pleiku or that we would flee to Saigon, so Fox giving me his information seemed strange. It added a hint of mystery to our unusual relationship.

I put the scrap of paper in my purse, just in case we happened to cross paths again. And after that night, I didn't give the dinner with Fox or the contact information stashed in my purse another thought— at least not until I arrived in Saigon months later in a panic. I was, after all, a happily married woman ... or so, I thought.

When I met Binh, I was nineteen years old—a rebellious teenager who'd only just begun to experience the freedom of adulthood. It was 1971 and my growing need for independence, as well as a recent disagreement with my father, had brought me on a personal journey of discovery from Da Lat to Pleiku.

My half-sister lived away from home and worked for Air America in Nha Trang, a town about sixty miles west of Da Lat. Knowing I was looking for a summer job, she recommended I interview for a position she had heard about in Pleiku. The job requirements were simple, she said. Applicants had to be presentable, have a high school education and understand some basic English. I passed each of those tests ... barely. And thanks to my sister's connections, Air America would fly me roundtrip to Pleiku for free.

Not knowing exactly what the job required, who it was with or what it would pay, I agreed to go just for the opportunity to escape the stern look of my father, if only for a day. I scheduled an interview and eagerly packed an overnight bag. I took just the necessities—a change of clothes and my makeup.

The trip from Da Lat to Pleiku was a one-hour Cessna flight north. It was the first time I had ever seen my hometown from the air. Rising over the clouds and green mountaintops, I felt the nervous exhilaration of freedom. It seemed we were airborne for only a few minutes before the plane began its gradual descent.

As we neared our destination, everything appeared flatter and less vibrant than the lush landscape of Da Lat. Rough on the edges but beautiful in its own way, this was Pleiku.

Some said there was no reason to be in Pleiku unless you absolutely had to be. It was true that most of the city's inhabitants either worked for the military or served those who did. I soon learned I was interviewing for a job working with American intelligence. This didn't faze me a bit. I had no idea what it meant.

When I arrived at a small military compound near the center of town, I was greeted by a large American I would only ever know or refer to as Mr. Houston. He was the boss in charge of overseeing all the department's operations. He was the only person who interviewed me.

Mr. Houston may or may not have been his real name. I was too young and clueless to realize he was C.I.A. His questions were straightforward and designed to judge my competency. He quizzed me on basic math—minus the plum and pickle treats—and the English alphabet, as well as on speaking and understanding easy words and phrases like "yes, thank you" and "no, thank you"—all of which I had learned by completing a basic English course through a company called English 4 Today.

Then he took me on a tour of the compound where I would be working, which was made up of three nondescript buildings with a courtyard in the middle. The place could have been mistaken for any other set of office buildings, had it not been for the perimeter edged in razor-wire fencing.

At the tour's conclusion, I followed Mr. Houston to a lounge where I heartily accepted a complimentary meal. The food was probably just an MRE (military speak for "meal ready to eat"), but to me it was an exotic and oddly delicious gourmet delight. While he reviewed my paperwork, I savored a can of franks-and-beans and watched an American movie, starring actors I had never seen, who were speaking a language I could not follow. *Wow,* I thought. *This is cool!*

An hour later, I was offered a job, though its duties and requirements were still completely unknown to me. I was told I could start immediately and would earn 12,000 Vietnamese *piastres* a month, which was about forty U.S. dollars in 1971. This I understood and quickly accepted. "Yes, thank you!"

I flew home to Da Lat the next morning to pack and say my goodbyes.

A few days later, back in Pleiku, my job responsibilities were finally laid out for me. They weren't half as exciting as the free hot dog dinner, Coke and movie.

All I would do was sit in a windowless, eight-square-foot room for eight hours a day (with one hour for lunch), six days a week and listen to the radio. But not one that played music. The giant, overheating console I tended was a communications hub used to connect one military office with another based on a simple, yet secret, number code. One caller would say, "This is one-two-three. I need to speak with four-five-six, please."

And I would patch the caller through. I was basically a silent switchboard operator. I didn't know what any of the numbers meant or who these people were; therefore, my job didn't require much talking or any special clearance.

It was not the most interesting work, but since this was more or less an American operation, it paid much better than any Vietnamese organization could afford. I was able to earn the money I needed to live on my own. It was in this dull office, with fewer than ten employees, that I would meet and get to know my first husband.

I met Binh the day I moved to Pleiku. He was designated my apartment-hunting guide and drove me around town in a Jeep (which, I was impressed to learn, was his own vehicle) to see some available rooms for rent. Because he knew the local area and spoke Chinese, English and Vietnamese, he helped me deal more easily with prospective landlords. I didn't know yet that he was actually the office manager—and my immediate supervisor—who reported to Mr. Houston.

Like everything else about my relocation experience, I decided on a place to live quickly. The first room we looked at was a little too expensive and too far from the office. I didn't want to incur the added expense of taking a bus or *cyclo* to work each day. Instead, I settled on a modest room in the second house we visited. It was perfectly located near the central market and just a few blocks from my office, making my walk to work mercifully short. This was crucial, since I went everywhere in a proper *Áo Dài* dress, balanced atop high heels.

My new home was about the size of a typical American bathroom—eight square feet, and just big enough to accommodate a single cot, chair, flickering lamp and clothes rack. The room didn't have a closet. It was the closet. Not that I had many clothes to wear anyway. I shared the even smaller bathroom downstairs with the other tenants and the landlords—a pleasant, middle-aged couple. To shower, I had to carry a bucket to the communal bathroom, stand in it and pour water over my head with a ladle. The sink for brushing teeth and washing faces was outdoors. It was not much, but for just 3,000 *piastres* a month (about twelve dollars U.S.), it was all mine!

The fact that Binh was fluent in several languages made him a valuable asset to the Americans and an easy choice to be the liaison between Vietnamese and U.S. intelligence. Obviously, he was smart. And like other women did, I thought he was very handsome. But I was not looking for any relationship. Being away from home for the first time, I savored my independence.

After a short time working together, however, an odd courtship began between us. Binh's secretary Khanh was in love with him. I knew this because Khanh and I were friends, and she told me so. A week after my arrival, she arranged for the three of us to go to the movie theater. I thought she was shy and wanted someone else to tag along for her date with Binh. Whatever her reasoning, I enjoyed going to the movies and was happy to have something to do in this new town where I didn't know anyone.

When Binh's Jeep pulled up to my house that evening, Khanh was not with him. I asked about her, and he said we would stop at her place on the way to the theater. Though it seemed a little strange that he picked me up first, I didn't give it much more thought. When we arrived at Khanh's house, she suddenly had another commitment and could not go with us. I thought it was all a coincidence. But in fact, Binh had asked Khanh to set us up.

This was our first date, even if I didn't know it. Afterwards, Binh and I began regularly showing up at the same places. This was his way of courting me in the traditional, passive-aggressive style of the Vietnamese man. Most often, Binh would meet me for lunch at a nearby restaurant that catered almost exclusively to the young soldiers who flocked there for its cheap, three-course meals. Because I had no kitchen of my own, I ate lunch and dinner there almost every day, usually alone and in full dress and makeup. Being that I was often the only girl daring enough to squeeze herself into a place packed wall-to-wall with men in uniform, I attracted plenty of attention.

The first time Binh saw me there—eating by myself, innocent and surrounded—he offered to keep me company. Although I was becoming skilled at blocking unwanted advances from strange men, I welcomed Binh's presence, if only to help scare off undesirables. And because he owned a Jeep, I liked that I could always count on him for a ride home, which helped me save a lot on *cyclo* fare.

Though our interactions were more practical than social in nature, Binh quickly graduated from bodyguard and chauffer to something more. Within a few weeks, we started going to nicer places together—to eat, drink and dance. We were officially "dating."

Vietnamese men rarely say "I love you." They aren't typically so direct. When their feelings for a woman grow stronger, they just begin showering her with more attention. My brother was a perfect example. As a teenager, he went to an all-boys school and fell in love with a neighbor who attended an all-girls school. He would stand outside the girl's house and gaze longingly at her through a window while she studied. From time to time, he would borrow a book from her and, before returning it, he would write a poem and slide it inside, pressed against a pansy. This is how Vietnamese boys court schoolgirls, and it's not a romantic strategy they abandon in adulthood. Even as grown men, they rarely come right out and express their intentions. Thus, Binh didn't say "I love you." He just asked me out for noodles more often.

In Vietnam, after two people have a few dates, the relationship is considered serious and, therefore, bound by certain expectations. In my generation, good Vietnamese girls grew up innocently believing that kissing could get them pregnant and that they must remain virgins until their wedding nights. So kissing was out of the question, and young brides believed they should only sleep with one man for the rest of their lives. After being "taken advantage of" by a man (which, in Vietnamese society, could mean holding hands or a getting a peck on the cheek), marriage was thought to be a woman's only option for restoring her honor. Given this mythology, small signs of affection carried great significance. Proper courtship mostly involved spending time together, sharing longing glances and whispering sweet nothings.

Although I had no physical contact with Binh during those first few weeks, it didn't take long for me to feel a strong connection with him. It was said back then that only two things were important to Vietnamese men: war and women. On the surface, Binh was no different. Though his job immersed him in conflict, he could be very romantic, and his most endearing quality was the way he treated me with great respect. I was this young woman who worked the switchboard in his office, yet he treated me as an equal rather than a subordinate.

Binh had many other personal qualities I valued: strength, confidence, wisdom and a love of family. In my youthful eyes, he was ideal. Right away, I knew Binh would be my husband.

In my parents' eyes, however, Binh was not a worthy choice, though they would never come right out and say it. Whether it was his chosen profession or something else that offended them, I sensed their obvious displeasure but found it hard to understand why they would question my judgment. Despite their concerns, in my mind, Binh and I were seriously committed and there was no turning back. After dating for three months, Binh and I got married.

As in most cultures, the typical Vietnamese wedding is an extravagant, joyous spectacle. But Binh and I exchanged our vows in a small, low-key ceremony with just a few family members in attendance. Nothing spoke louder of my parents' opposition than that.

A few months later, I had moved into Binh's house and was pregnant with our first child. Bang was born on March 30, 1972, and soon after, I quit my full-time job to stay home and raise a family. Binh's townhouse, sophisticated by the standards of the day, was more like a long, narrow, single-story flat—with a ten-square-foot living room, small kitchen, single bedroom and bathroom with indoor plumbing. It was a giant leap forward in accommodations from my small boardinghouse room. Later, after we had children, we even hired a housekeeper to help me cook and clean.

Although I had quit my switchboard job, I did work a few days a week with one of the local political parties as an executive assistant and event planner. All in all, I thought I was living a normal life—a good life, even.

In early 1975, when Binh and I had been married for almost four years, everything changed. That year ushered in the tough life my grandmother feared I would have, and neither she nor the stars could do anything to help me avoid it. By springtime, two different enemies would invade my "normal" Central Highlands existence, almost simultaneously and with equal devastation for me. One was the North Vietnamese Army (NVA); the other was the "other woman."

Faith and spirituality have helped me through most of my life's difficult events and changes. During that extraordinary spring of 1975, I remember thinking there really must be a divine plan for me. At least I hoped there was, and I suppose that's what faith is all about. But as with all divine plans, most of the details would only become clear in hindsight—and some not until decades later.

As the chaos unfolded, I vaguely sensed I was being guided, but I had no clue as to what it all meant or where it would lead me. The only thing I knew for sure was this: the critical first step would be to get my children out of Vietnam.

Chapter 3: *War and Women*

Mai was born in November 1974 in Da Lat. I had gone there to stay with family for the final weeks of my pregnancy, just as I had with my son Bang. In December, when I returned to Pleiku, everything seemed as safe and serene as I had left it.

On one of my first days back in town, while shopping at the local market, I ran into a friend standing outside a cosmetics shop. As the girlfriend of Pleiku's mayor, she was privy to all the local political and military activity, and she was eager to catch me up on news I had missed while away. Among other gossip, we discussed a rumor that the Viet Cong (VC) was already advancing on Ban Me Thuot (located about 100 miles south of us) and what this might mean for Pleiku's immediate future. Another friend, whose husband was an Army colonel in charge of an elite fighting unit on its way to Ban Me Thuot for battle, overheard us and confirmed the rumor to be true.

I was silent for a minute and thought, Could we be next? It hardly seemed possible the war could touch us, especially with such a formidable American military presence in town. When I asked my friends what they planned to do if we had to evacuate Pleiku, both said they'd go to Saigon to stay with family until the fighting subsided. As the capital of South Vietnam, it was well fortified and considered the safest part of the country.

Without knowing the fall of Saigon was just five months away, my friends and I still considered hostilities near Pleiku to be more of an inconvenience than a real threat to our security. We were used to hearing about the war being fought elsewhere—in the jungles, other towns or different regions of the country. If it happened to come to our area, we assumed it would pass through as quickly as a summer storm.

Until hearing about Ban Me Thuot, we had all been fairly confident.

Trees might bend and shed leaves, but the war winds would diminish, clouds would clear, and life would soon return to normal. The three of us parted ways feeling uneasy and wondering how long it would be before we knew our fate. In the back of my mind, I wondered if I should prepare an evacuation plan.

A few months later, Binh was called away to Saigon. His commanders there needed his report on enemy activity in the Central Highlands. For this kind of debriefing trip, he was usually gone a few days. He left on a Thursday in late March. That Sunday, while Binh was still out of town, the storm front my friends and I had downplayed suddenly swept into Pleiku.

I walked to mass that morning running later than usual. Thinking I could get there more quickly on my own, I left the kids at home with our housekeeper and my brother-in-law. As I approached the church, I didn't see the typical overflowing crowd or hear the hymns that usually played as I walked up the front steps. Today it was quiet. I wondered, *Am I really that late?*

Inside I found the sanctuary less than half filled. Assuming I had missed the service, I quickly knelt in the shadows to cross myself and then started home.

On my way out, my friend Dinh stopped me on the sidewalk and nearly shouted, "Why are you still here?"

"What do you mean?" I asked, confused by her panic. "I'm just on my way home from church."

"We're leaving right now, because the VC is at our doorstep," she said. "The Americans have pulled out. The South Vietnamese Army is gone too. Region II moved out of town last night. There's nobody left to hold the VC back. Thuong, you need to find a way to get out!"

I tried to process what she was saying. *How am I going to get my kids out? My husband is gone. I'm here alone.* Thank God for Dinh. Had I skipped my usual Sunday routine, I would have missed her early warning.

I ran to see my friend An, whose husband worked in Binh's office and whose family owned a restaurant in town. I told An what Dinh told me, and while I waited at the restaurant, she went to check on available flights at the Air Vietnam ticket counter down the street. She was shocked to find ticket prices for flights out of town had skyrocketed from 1,000 to more than 50,000 *piastres*, which was about $250 U.S. and several times more than a typical Vietnamese worker's annual wage. Even at this criminal price, there were no tickets left. Clearly only those with military connections had any chance of finding alternate transportation out of town.

An rushed off to find her husband, and I left to get my kids. Hurrying out of the restaurant, I bumped into Phuong, another friend who happened to be a helicopter pilot in the South Vietnamese Air Force. Already that day, someone had offered him several thousand U.S. dollars, under the table, for a flight out of town. I had almost no cash in my purse, but I asked for his help anyway, hoping he might let us stow away on his next flight to Nha Trang, the main naval base in South Vietnam. It was about 125 miles southeast of Pleiku—not out of the country, but out of harm's way for the moment. I hoped this would allow me time to find Binh in Saigon.

"I'll give you exactly thirty minutes to pack," Phuong said. "But pack lightly." He agreed to fly my children and me out, asking for nothing in return. Again I thanked God, because other than my eternal gratitude, "nothing" was about all I had to offer him for such priceless emergency transport. A half hour was barely enough time for me to run home. Knowing there would not be much room for anything but the four of us in Phuong's helicopter, I grabbed only a few essential items.

Phuong arrived to pick us up just as I was stuffing a cloth diaper into my shoulder bag. He got us safely to the Nha Trang airport where, with help from my sister's Air America coworker, I secured a flight for the final leg to Saigon. This was yet another blessing to be counted. Had I not stumbled into Phuong on the sidewalk, it's likely that my children and I, like thousands of other desperate souls fleeing the Central Highlands, would have had no choice but to risk our lives on a long, perilous march out of town.

Later I would learn that more than 100,000 exhausted men, women and children walked from Pleiku to Saigon. Fathers hauled as many family possessions as they could, while mothers clutched their children, some still breastfeeding, as they staggered through a near-constant barrage of NVA artillery and VC ambushes. Two-thirds of them perished during the exodus now known to many Westerners as the "Convoy of Tears." The Vietnamese call it "The Blood Road."

When we finally made it to my mother-in-law's home in Saigon, I discovered that Binh had left for Pleiku to find us. Heading in opposite directions, we probably passed each other at Nha Trang's airport. There was no word yet from my family, who were also in danger in Da Lat. They may have been traveling to Saigon or even out of the country. There was no way to know, since I could not contact any of them. I could only pray for their safety and wait.

Biding time in Saigon was difficult for many reasons. One was my mother-in-law. Although welcoming, she was completely unprepared to provide room and board for my children and me, and she certainly did not have the means to sustain us for an extended stay. To make matters worse, I had very little money and no way to help support my family. But the most frustrating thing about being in Saigon without Binh was not knowing where he was or whether he would ever make it back.

Adding to my uneasiness and worry were rumors of another kind that I had started to hear a few months earlier. While in Pleiku just after Mai was born, I heard talk about Binh being seen with another woman. Unfortunately, it was not the first time I had heard this and been tempted to question his fidelity. But given the extreme circumstances, I had chosen to ignore the stories. Now I was in Saigon, panicked and virtually alone and unsure how to feel about his absence. I started to analyze details of his past business trips and TDY assignments. I wondered, *Has he been honest with me?* These seeds of doubt diverted my attention from what should have been my only concern during such a crisis: the safety of my children. This made me angry with myself.

While my anxiety grew with each passing hour that brought no word from Binh, my confidence and self-esteem eroded just as quickly. I began to feel I had become a burden to Binh's family in Saigon and worry that I might not be the provider my children required. I needed help. It was then I remembered the little slip of paper given to me by Fox. I decided to go look for him and ask for his help.

Very few people in Vietnam at that time could afford to have phones in their homes, even in a major city like Saigon. My mother-in-law was not one of those people. Although Fox had given me the number for his office in downtown Saigon, it was of no use to me. If I wanted to talk to him, I would have to do so in person.

I emptied the contents of my purse to find the slip of paper with Fox's Saigon address and retrieve what little cash I had saved. I had maybe a few thousand *piastres*, which wasn't a lot even before the currency's value began to plummet in 1975. But it was enough to get a ride into the city. I put on makeup and a proper dress for going downtown, left my children with their grandmother and hailed a *cyclo*.

The New York Times office was stuck in the middle of a row of low-rise buildings. My *cyclo* pulled up in front of the one bearing the same numbers printed on the piece of paper Fox had given me. In high heels, I gingerly stepped onto the curb, shuffled to the building's unmarked glass door and pushed my way inside. Harsh sunlight surrendered to shadow, momentarily blinding me, as I stood blinking in the middle of the broom-closet-sized lobby. After climbing a few flights of stairs, I emerged from the stairwell to find a man confined behind a reception desk adorned with only a modest sign indicating this was the right place. There was another door behind him.

"Is Mr. Fox here, please?" I asked before being politely told to have a seat. I didn't have an appointment. I was just some strange, nearly hysterical girl who'd shown up at Fox's office out of the blue.

With all that had happened during the past few weeks, I had not been able to think things through, so I had not prepared what to say and didn't know what to expect from Fox when I actually came face to face with him again. All I knew for sure was that he had given me his contact information, so he must have meant for me to use it. I eased myself onto a well-worn bench near the doorway, trying to suppress equal feelings of dread, anxiety and confusion in order to regain my balance.

Fox appeared within a few minutes. His face showed concern but, just as he had at dinner months before, he exuded a sense of calm.

Before he could say anything, I cried in frustration, "I have no job and no money. Binh is gone. I don't know what to do. My kids..."

Fox seemed to somehow understand that I was not asking for a handout. I needed someone to hear me. Even though I barely knew him, I felt I could trust Fox. He had traveled all over the world and was, I assumed, very well connected and powerful.

He paused for a moment, looking into my eyes. His kind gaze helped me focus and eased my nerves. "Wait here," he said. "I'll be right back."

After disappearing into a back office, he returned with something clenched in his hand. It was money—maybe 25,000 *piastres*, about $100 U.S., which was a lot of money in those days, even for Americans. For me it was a small fortune.

Some might view this as a typical solution: throw money at the problem and make it go away. But Fox didn't simply shove cash in my hands and then shoo me out the door. Instead, he listened and showed me compassion. He didn't make me feel like I was imposing. He treated me with respect. Then he did something else I was not expecting. He gave me a hug. As bold as it was in the Vietnamese culture for a stranger to hug you, it was exactly the comfort I needed. I could not hold back any longer. For a long time, in the middle of *The New York Times* lobby, I cried in his arms.

Over the next few weeks, I occasionally visited Fox's office—just long enough to say hello, express my gratitude and let him know I would not take his kindness for granted. I considered the money he gave me a loan. Whether I could ever repay it, I was not sure. His generosity—something to which I was unaccustomed—taught me to be kind to others. I believed then as I do now that this kind of unconditional giving is as close to seeing God's face as it gets.

After a very long week, Binh finally showed up at his mother's house. On his way back from Pleiku, he had crossed paths with my parents in Nha Trang. They had given him their car, which he drove the rest of the way to Saigon. Just seeing him come through the front door was enough to erase nearly every doubt from my mind. I ran to him, elated he had made it back to see his children. We were all in the same city and a family again.

As happy and relieved as we were to be together, a sense of urgency remained. With the NVA advancing towards Saigon, Binh still needed a contingency plan in case the city fell into enemy hands. Every day after his return, Binh and I waited in line at the U.S. Embassy to get on the official list for departure. Even as we made this daily pilgrimage, we tried to retain some sense of normalcy in our lives.

We were told our evacuation orders would be coming within a matter of days, and this finally afforded us some time to relax. It turned out to be a short but much-needed respite, because the next few weeks would knock the wind out of me.

It was mid-April and we didn't know the fall of Saigon was just days away. While we awaited our departure orders, I went about my regular business of taking care of the children, looking for work and occasionally shopping. One afternoon I decided to go to the beauty salon before doing a little shopping (despite those uncertain times, I believed it was important for one to always look her best, especially when job hunting). After getting my hair and nails done, I hailed a taxi to take me to the market (no *cyclo* could protect my freshly styled hair). The taxi broke down on the way, and after several noisy minutes with the driver's head under the hood of the car, he told me it was a lost cause.

"You'll just have to find another way," he said. "You can walk or find a *cyclo*. Don't worry; the market isn't too far from here."

Easy for him to say. He was not the one who'd be navigating an unfamiliar city in heels while trying to protect a new hairdo. I didn't know where I was or which direction to go. This was a feeling with which I would soon become all too familiar.

As I looked around, I noticed a few small stores and restaurants along the street ahead. This was a scaled-back version of the main market, certainly, but at least the shops would provide some distraction and make the walk a little more pleasant. I had planned this as a window-shopping trip anyway, so I was happy to begin my casual browsing while on the way to my intended destination.

By scanning buildings and street signs, I hoped to get my bearings. Then I saw a familiar street name. I could not recall exactly where I had seen or heard it before, but I latched on to it like a lifeline. Then, as I stood on a corner trying to decide which way to turn, I solved the mystery. While picking some clothes up off our dresser weeks earlier, I accidentally knocked Binh's wallet to the floor. Money fell out of it, as well as a scrap of paper with an address printed in his handwriting. I assumed the address was business related and belonged to a colleague of his in Saigon.

Looking again at the sign overhead, I saw that the street names matched. With my small-town mentality, I was encouraged by the prospect of finding a friendly face—or at least someone who knew my husband—in this neighborhood. I hoped this friend of Binh's might help with directions to the market, or even have a phone I could use.

While I was now certain of the street name, the specific house number escaped me. After several minutes of walking past rows of unfamiliar houses and apartments, hoping something might help jog my memory, I had all but given up. Then I saw Binh's car parked on the street in front of a townhouse. My face lit up, and I innocently thought, *How lucky!*

The ground-floor entrance to the townhouse was open. Thrilled to have discovered Binh was off work early and could go shopping with me, or maybe even to see a movie, I walked in. I was beaming—all dressed up and in good spirits.

There was a woman—the cook—in the kitchen. When she greeted me, I told her I was there to see Binh. She said he was upstairs and that I could go right on up to the living room. Seeing how I was dressed, the cook must have thought I was there on business. Smiling, I thanked her and ascended the stairs, still wondering whose house this might be.

When I reached the living room on the main floor, I didn't see Binh anywhere. Across the room, past sparse furnishings, there was a closed door. I pushed open what turned out to be the bedroom door. Then my heart sank. On the bed, face-down, was Binh, and he was not alone.

With his back to the door, Binh didn't notice me enter the room and didn't stop what he was doing until his mistress tapped him on the shoulder. Then, too calmly, she said to me, "Please don't scream." There was little chance of that; I could barely breathe.

Binh became a blur as he bolted from the bed, almost as if he were not there at all, and disappeared into the bathroom, giving me a moment to compose myself. I needed more. The room suddenly got warmer. My vision briefly dimmed. I thought I was going to faint. It was well known in Vietnam that many married men (sadly, including some in my own family) kept women on the side. *Shouldn't I have known better?* I thought. *Shouldn't I have seen this coming?* I remembered the old saying: "For Vietnamese men, there is only war and women." But until you actually catch your husband—the father of your children—with another woman, the whispers you hear are rumors to dismiss. Is this my fault? I never wanted to take the gossip seriously, never wanted to let myself believe. Even in that room, I still didn't want to believe. What do I do now?

After making himself more presentable, Binh came out of the bathroom and said he wanted to take me home. I could not look at him. Seething, I said, "How could you?" over and over again. He kept insisting he should take me home, but I just stood frozen in this other woman's home, in her filthy room. "No," I said at last. "You go home!"

"Go, Binh," said the woman. "I will take her home."

Binh left. I stayed.

With him gone, I suddenly began to think very clearly. This woman and I had some things to discuss.

"Didn't you know this man was married?" I asked. "He has two children with me. What is the matter with you?"

Completely unruffled, she replied, "I knew, but I wanted to have a little fling. I mean, he's really good looking."

My anger must have thawed out my legs, because I had made my way over to the bureau next to the bed. Turning abruptly from her, I opened a few drawers to find several articles of Binh's clothing neatly folded inside, as if he lived there. The woman admitted they'd been seeing each other for more than a year. This was not just a "fling." I felt sick.

I really must have been in shock, because not only did I accept the woman's offer to give me a ride home, but I also invited her to come back that evening.

"I assume you know the family pretty well," I told her. "Why don't you come have dinner with us tonight?" I was testing her to see if she would have the guts to face Binh's family with me there. And I wanted to see their reactions.

That night, just as dinner was being put on the table, there was a knock on the door. It was her. *The nerve of this vile woman!* I thought, as I let her inside.

At the dinner table, I remained as calm as a wife could while seated across from her husband's mistress and his family—including his grandmother, who was well into her eighties. Just after the soup and before the noodles, I broke the conversational ice.

Pointing at her like a witness identifying a guilty defendant in a courtroom, I said, "This woman is having an affair with my husband, and I caught them today."

Silence.

I knew then that they were all aware and had done nothing about it. The meal was over. There was no dessert.

With the dinner party now spoiled, Binh and I left to speak in private. When we were alone, all the emotion I had suppressed in the company of his family and his mistress erupted in a single slap across his face.

"How dare you betray me and our children?!" I yelled.

He said he was sorry, but his words weren't nearly enough. I could not listen to him, much less ever be intimate with him again. That would make me feel dirty. I heard myself say he had ruined the sanctity of our marriage and killed the love I had for him. And that was that.

From that day forward, I put all my energy into finding a way out of Vietnam with my children. Waiting around with Binh for his evacuation orders to come through was no longer a good option for me. I needed a backup plan. My priority was to protect my kids. More and more, it looked like the only person we could rely on for help was not Binh or the South Vietnamese government; it was my friend, the American journalist.

Chapter 4: *Sink or Swim*

After his betrayal, I could not love Binh the same way I had before. But I was stuck. My children still needed him to be their father and, in our strict Vietnamese society, leaving him was simply not an option. In a more practical sense, I could not imagine life as a single parent. Would I go back to renting an eight-square-foot room and working six days a week in an office, like when I first moved to Pleiku? Even if I wanted to, how could I? With Bang and Mai to care for, those living conditions were no longer feasible.

I wanted to believe that if we could just leave Vietnam as a family, with cooler heads and less chaos clouding our judgment, maybe we could work everything out. It was with this mindset that I prepared to spend my final days in Saigon with my husband.

Because his position gave him access to inside information, Binh knew May 11th was the absolute deadline for all American military personnel and civilians to evacuate Saigon. Our relocation, along with the other South Vietnamese military families, was allegedly scheduled for no later than May 10th. With this date nearly a month away, we assumed we had ample time to prepare for departure. We were wrong.

Binh and I went to the U.S. Embassy travel office each morning as the May 11th deadline (and the NVA) steadily approached. We waited in line for hours, hoping to get our official orders and travel documents. But each day, like thousands of others eager to put the war behind them, we were told to come back tomorrow.

One day, as we stood in line going nowhere, something caught my eye, interrupting a perfectly good daydream. Actually, it was someone—Binh's mistress. She was standing off to the side with her daughter, leaning against a wall just as casually and confidently as the day she'd come to the house for dinner on the day I caught them. My stomach tightened. Binh must have promised to take them with him—with us. It was clear that nothing would stand in the way of his affair with her. Not me, not the war, not even his family.

Until I saw her standing there, I had clung to the notion that if Binh and I could spend more time together and calmly work through our troubles, eventually we could repair our marriage. But discovering she was still in his plans was the last straw. It was time for me to pursue my backup plan of escape, or the kids and I might just wake up one day and discover that Binh had left without us.

The next day, I paid my final visit to the Saigon office of *The New York Times*.

Americans were free to come and go at their leisure during the war, unlike the Vietnamese citizens, who had to contend with a complex bureaucracy and paperwork before they could leave the country. The Vietnamese, however, knew Americans could sponsor refugees and get them out with relative ease. Most believed they could emigrate with a sponsor even without a passport. This may have been true a few months earlier. But I knew as soon as White Christmas played on Armed Forces Radio—the code which signaled all remaining American officials and citizens to evacuate—that safe passage for Vietnamese refugees would become infinitely more complicated and expensive, if not impossible. So for the first time, I had come to Fox for more than encouraging words and a shoulder to cry on.

Once Fox and I were safely behind his closed office door, I got right to the point. I blurted, "Can you take me and my children out of the country?"

I had never been so forward. If he could not hear the desperation in my voice, he must have seen it on my face. I knew he was not married, so I didn't think my question had crossed any personal boundaries. He opened his mouth to speak but stopped short of saying anything. Taking a moment to get his thoughts in order, he sighed and began to search his desk for a notepad. With the precision of a teletype, he jotted down some information and handed it to me. It was the address of his apartment in Saigon—not something he would give to just anyone. For whatever reason—out of kindness, mercy or even love—he let me know I had a way out.

Binh disappeared on the morning of April 30. We were supposed to be picked up at a designated rendezvous point by someone from the U.S. Embassy and leave together as a family. I assumed he had gone ahead to ensure arrangements were in order and that we should just meet him there. But when I arrived at the pickup area, with Bang and Mai squirming in my arms, there were two problems. First, the place was empty, its doors locked. Second, Binh was not there.

I knew that Binh, like me, had become impatient with the official evacuation process and had begun exploring alternatives for leaving the country. He was a soldier, after all, and if he was caught by the NVA, his fate would be a war prison camp ... or worse. While I believed he deserved to face the consequences for his marital transgressions, he didn't deserve the brutality that surely awaited him upon capture. If he had found another way out and seized the opportunity, I would have understood—even if it meant using his mistress's connections. She worked for a French company and had a dual citizenship, which offered him a possible escape route into Europe.

I left the rendezvous point and, on a hunch, took a *cyclo* to his mistress's house. Entering her house was like walking back into a bad dream I had been trying to repress. It was not a place I ever wanted to see again. This time I called out his name to announce myself. There was no response.

I continued up to the second level, my legs quivering with each step. As before, the living room was empty and silent. I was no longer thinking.

My footsteps were automatic; my legs moved of their own accord and carried me towards the bedroom. After nudging open the door, I hesitated to cross its threshold. But I didn't need to enter. From across the room, I could see the message Binh had left for her, scrawled on the mirror above her dresser in lipstick: I love you and miss you.

She must have seen the note, wasted no time making herself up and run to be with him. I was shocked. In the worst of circumstances, with the world falling down, this was where he decided to go first. He had given this expression of love to her—not his wife or children. And now she would be the one who got to say goodbye to him. I felt the anger welling from deep within me. I wanted to scream.

I had moved out of Binh's parents' house the previous week, taking the kids with me to stay at my aunt's house in Saigon. Also staying there were my parents and all my brothers and sisters, who'd recently arrived from Da Lat. My aunt was married to the New Zealand journalist Peter Arnett, whom she had met while studying abroad. He was covering the war for the *Associated Press*, and they had evacuated Saigon weeks before with many other news organizations, leaving their home available to us.

Unlike my mother-in-law, the Arnetts had a phone. On April 30, that phone rang. It was Binh's mistress. No matter how hard I tried to rid my life of this woman, she continued to find me. Annoyed though I was, what she had to say was worth the momentary aggravation.

"Your husband is on a boat. He leaves today. You should go meet him down at the port."

I didn't understand. Why the port? Why not the airport? As she explained where I was to meet Binh, all I could think was, Here I am, soon to be stranded in Saigon with a three-year-old and six-month-old clinging to me. And I'm being told by my husband's mistress to go search for him among a crowd of thousands ... on a boat!

Leaving him may not have been possible from a cultural standpoint but, realistically and emotionally, our marriage was finished. I cleared my head. There was no time to feel jealous or hurt. Bang and Mai needed me. We were all in danger and on our own to find a way out.

First, I have to take the kids to see him off, I told myself. They should say goodbye. I hoped there might even be a chance Binh would take his son with him. Regardless of what kind of boat Binh was on— a cargo ship, battleship or dingy—our infant daughter was too young for that kind of travel. She needed to stay on land with me.

I asked my brother to take us down to the port. Minh was a lieutenant in the South Vietnamese Army, which enabled him to travel freely. But like my husband, his service also guaranteed a long prison term or even a death sentence if captured. With my mother's help, I convinced him to try and find a place on an outbound boat after dropping us off. Once he agreed to the plan, I stuffed a couple essentials—a diaper and bottle of milk—into a handbag, scooped up my kids and rushed out the door.

Minh weaved his way through traffic down to the Port of Saigon with me, Bang and Mai perched unsteadily on his Vespa scooter. When we got there, we saw pure madness—a sea of too many people bottlenecked at too few pier gates while thousands of desperate bodies crested over gangplanks and all sizes and varieties of watercrafts lined up to ferry people away to safety. Finding Binh in this human tsunami would be next to impossible, so I told Minh to leave us at one of the piers and then make his own escape. I would look for Binh myself and find a way home later.

The Vespa sputtered away, leaving me and the children in a puff of black exhaust. I suddenly felt very alone. A *cyclo* cabbie must have seen us standing in the middle of the confusion, all three of us crying. He offered to take us anywhere we wanted to go. I asked for a ride to another, less-crowded pier. "We're looking for their father," I explained. "And I'm not sure which boat he's on."

Thousands of other people were also there looking—many for loved ones and all of them for a way out. Had we not been seated in the *cyclo,* the crowds surely would have swallowed us and we never would have made it to the next pier. The cabbie pedaled furiously ahead, dodging the people and *cyclos* swarming past us in all directions. The surreal scene flickered by me like one of the old black-and-white newsreels played before Hollywood films.

The next pier had a gate secured by two serious-looking soldiers and crowned with ribbons of barbed wire. An unruly mob pushed to get in, while people wildly pleaded their cases for why they deserved to go through. Many tried bribing the guards to let them pass. I had nothing of value to offer, but I approached the gate anyway. Because I was well-dressed, had two young children in tow and was still noticeably upset, the guard greeted me with an unusually friendly look and gave us his full attention. Half expecting to be brushed aside, I told the guard I was looking for my husband so he could say goodbye to his children. The guard looked at me and then at my kids, then quickly waved us through without requiring a toll.

The pier was not as crowded as several others we had seen. And on this side of the gate, though still loud and packed with people, it was a bit calmer at the moment. Everyone here seemed prepared for the long journey. People stood dutifully with luggage stacked neatly beside them. Every once in a while, someone would shoot me a puzzled glance, as if wondering why a mother with two kids would be waiting there without the father or even a single suitcase.

I found out later why all these people were still waiting and not scrambling to board the ship. They had been told to stay put until the captain returned. Apparently, he had gone home to retrieve his own family and luggage.

Most of the travelers were concentrated at one end of the pier, leaving an open area on the other side. This allowed me, Bang and Mai to stand apart from the crowd, which I hoped would give Binh a better chance of spotting us, particularly if he happened to be standing on the ship's deck two stories above.

From here I could see a few naval ships in port, all of which were filled to near overflowing. There were countless more refugees trying to jump onto whatever boat still had space available—including river barges, fishing boats and repurposed vessels like the tanker in front of me. As long as it floated, the desperate would not complain.

Of all the different kinds of boats Binh could have chosen, an oil tanker would be the last thing I expected. As the number of hopeful evacuees on the pier steadily grew, I shuffled farther down, trying to maintain some distance between us and the churning crowd. Mai was in my arms, and Bang was just ahead of us.

The tanker, its massive hull buffeted by waves made by the many other vessels hastily exiting port, sloshed back and forth, often knocking up against the large splintered bumpers that protected the weathered concrete pier. There was a heavy chop in the water, which made it hard for the crew to drop the gangplank where they wanted—a spot farther up the pier where most everyone was anxiously waiting to board. After what seemed like hours of scanning the ship's railing high above me, as well as the sea of faces around me, looking for Binh, I heard the gangplank fall. It landed right at my son's feet.

The next thing I saw was Bang in his blue jeans, toddling excitedly towards the ramp like it was his own personal red carpet, beckoning him to begin a great adventure.

One of the crew members saw Bang and rushed down to meet him on the dock. Thinking he was doing me a favor by helping us board the ship ahead of the impending rush of evacuees, the sailor scooped Bang into his arms and hurried up the ramp, calling to me over his shoulder, "Come quickly—this way, miss!"

I froze in disbelief. We weren't supposed to be leaving, not like this. "Wait!" I called. "That's my kid! Come back!"

Frantic, I ran after them. By the time I reached Bang and explained my situation to the helpful crewman, a sea of humanity had begun pouring onto the ship. About twenty minutes and more than 1,000 anxious passengers later, the kids and I were far from the entrance, and the gangplank had been raised.

I told anyone who would listen that I had to get off the ship. All I got in response was, "Okay, jump in and swim."

As the pier receded and the boat turned towards its destination, I could see other families standing at the edge of the pier, arms outstretched to the departing ship as if it were a loved one torn from their embrace.

Minutes later, gunfire rang out from somewhere down the pier. It appeared the military (I'm not sure whose) was trying to disperse the crowd. Was it "friendly fire" to allow the ship to pull away, or was it the beginning of another slaughter? Things became more confused as the soldiers continued to make their point by firing warning shots into the air above the crowd.

As the tanker retreated from the pier, I thought, *What is happening to us?* We had set sail without my husband and even without the ship's captain. My heart raced to keep up as the whole scene played out before me. This moment required a split-second decision, and none of my options were ideal. But like many other choices I had faced during those final days in Vietnam, this one was made for me. Even if the kids and I survived jumping overboard, I didn't know how to swim. So I stayed put and hoped the tanker stayed afloat.

The gunfire on the pier launched me into survival mode and sent me in search of shelter on the crowded deck. As I sidestepped mounds of luggage and dodged dazed passengers, a familiar face emerged from the crowd. It belonged to one of my brother's friends, someone I knew as Lieutenant Hoe. Although he seemed distracted, I could tell he also recognized me. He quickly greeted me and said he was looking for his wife. Under one arm, he hugged a suitcase she had packed. He gave me a farewell nod before wandering off to resume his mission.

Navigating the sprawling deck like a *cyclo* through a congested market, I was able to claim one of the few remaining open spaces—a low-lying area near the ship's bow and against a wall. Hoping it was enough to protect us from any future military attacks, I felt my body wilt against the hard dampness of the wall as I cradled Mai in my lap and corralled Bang into the crook of one arm. It may have been due to the unwelcoming chill of the tanker's hull or simple fear, but I felt a tremble ripple through Bang's body. Or maybe it was mine.

The echo of pistol and rifle cracks subsided as we headed downriver from Saigon towards the South China Sea. Suddenly the sporadic shots gave way to a torrent of enemy rockets aimed at the soldiers on the pier, as well as those of us on the tanker. A screech of projectiles pierced the air, and the sky began to fall. A few of the explosions rocked the deck. It didn't make sense. Why were they shooting at us? This was not a war ship, and we weren't soldiers.

Minutes into the bombardment, something screamed over our heads. I ducked to shield Bang and Mai with my body. There was an explosion. Then another. Everyone and everything around me shook. There was more screaming. Cries from passengers—both the wounded and the hysterical—were mixed with the sound of rockets cutting through the darkening sky.

The smell of sulfur burned in my nostrils and stabbed at my throat as I lifted my head to survey the damage. Once the ringing in my ears subsided, I heard a hissing sound above me. A foot-long piece of shrapnel had embedded itself inches from my head, where it now sizzled like a branding iron.

I heard from others that a famous Vietnamese writer was killed during the attack. One of many casualties inflicted by the mortar rounds, he had not been on deck but sheltered in the relative comfort of the ship's interior when a direct hit wiped him from existence. A victim of war's random destruction, not even his fame and privilege could ensure his safety.

I pried loose the jagged hunk of metal over my head and put it in my purse, deciding to keep it as a reminder of how lucky I had been. The attack was over, but I remained alert. I pulled my precious children closer, gently urging them to keep their heads down. I did not want them to see our boat, its hull tilting dramatically to one side and taking on water at an unknown rate, or the mortally wounded bodies drifting out to sea with the current. None of the passengers would be able to rest until we had reached a friendly port. And none of us knew when that might be.

As we drifted down the river, I thought about what I had just left behind. My situation was the same as the millions of other families ripped apart by the war. But in some ways, it was different. In just a few weeks, my marriage had crumbled like the world around me. Several twists of fate had somehow nudged us aboard this westbound tanker. Our attempt to say goodbye to Binh had failed. In fact, we had not said goodbye to anyone. Now it was just the three of us, shivering on a boat, unprepared and headed towards the unknown.

Maybe I should have felt fortunate that my children were safe. I can only imagine what horrors we might have endured had we not made it out when we did. I'm still saddened to know that thousands of other families, mothers and children were unable to avoid the tragedy of war.

Years later I learned that Binh missed his ship because he decided to go back to my aunt's house for us. To this day, I don't know exactly why he returned. I hope it was because he loved us. When Binh asked my mother where his wife and children were, she screamed, "She went looking for you! You've killed my daughter!" His choice to return earned him thirteen hard years in a prison camp.

When Binh and I finally met again almost fifteen years later, he asked me to forgive him. I told him that forgiveness was between him and God, that I had remarried and moved on. And if he truly loved me and his children, he should return to his current wife and stay faithful to her. I advised him to go back to college so that he could have an easier life. I wanted him to be proud of himself—to be someone his children would admire. To his credit, he took my advice, went back to school and has achieved all of that.

I was not able to contact any of the family I left behind for more than five years, until the Vietnamese government finally opened up its borders to international mail service. For many years, my mother, father, brothers and sisters thought my children and I had been killed during the bombardment at the port. I didn't actually see any of them for several more years. In 1985, my brother Phong and father made it to the U.S. with the help of my half-sister in Norfolk, Virginia. I was able to sponsor my mother and three of my younger siblings—two brothers and a sister—another five years later in 1990.

The war, with all its many brutalities and levels of devastation, eventually did "pass through," but not nearly as quickly and inconsequentially as my Pleiku friends and I had thought it would. And what it left behind was not at all what we expected. There was no peace, no quiet and no normal life to which any of us could return.

Like a manmade tsunami, war obliterates everything. And no matter who "wins," everyone is a victim. Everyone is left scarred. In war's aftermath, how does anyone on either side, military or civilian, maintain goodness in his or her heart? How can anyone remain at all innocent, hopeful or positive? Once the fighting subsides, it's easy to allow ourselves to become bitter and angry. But because of the consideration others showed me during my journey out of the darkness of Vietnam, I've been able to hang on to my belief that kindness, compassion and love can conquer all—even war.

Chapter 5: *Adrift*

Accommodations aboard the ship weren't hospitable. This was an oil tanker, which typically operated with a crew of just twenty-five. Now it was transporting these men and more than 1,000 castaways. Its interior barely provided enough sheltered quarters for a skeleton crew, their families and the select VIPs who'd managed to smooth-talk their way into the belly of the ship. This left most of the others out on the open deck in the blistering sun with their luggage.

The ship carried no milk (although some of the more prepared passengers had packed some food and milk for themselves) and only a limited supply of water and rice rations—enough, perhaps, to sustain a small crew and a few hundred refugees for a few days, but not nearly enough for the actual number of people aboard. And in our damaged vessel, the voyage would take at least a week or two on open sea. Just like the grueling process of obtaining our evacuation papers, this meant waiting in long, unruly lines and hoping to reach the front before supplies were cut off for the day.

There was something else unavailable to me in the supply lines, something basic but almost as important as milk to a young mother traveling with an infant—diapers. I had put just one spare in my purse before leaving my aunt's house (I only planned to be gone for a short time). So every few hours, I had to use a faucet near the deck's edge to rinse out Mai's cloth diaper. With two young children, the chores began to make it very difficult.

Most of the other passengers were with family or were soldiers traveling in groups. They could take turns waiting in line for rations. Being the lone adult in my party, I either had to wait in line with my kids, which was difficult for us all, or make friends with reliable people who could watch them while I waited in line myself. Within the first day, I managed to ally myself with a half-dozen people who could help protect my kids and me—most of them men, whom I was able to woo with the promise: "If you help me, I'll marry you when we get to the port." These proposals were just the means to an end.

While many of those I encountered were very helpful, if at a price, it was discouraging to learn how some people treated their fellow human beings during a crisis. In our tight quarters, The Golden Rule seemed to dissolve in a solution of seawater and stress. People who were relatively well off and without urgent need of supplies hoarded what they had and refused to share with anyone, for any reason. Some childless passengers who had plenty of rations even refused to share with children. And when desperate people humbled themselves enough to ask these hoarders to spare even the smallest portion of their stash, they would simply lie and say they had nothing. It was a depressing reality, but that's just how some people act when they are forced out of their element, uncertain about the future and fighting for survival.

I felt as though I had been constantly looking for someplace safe since leaving Pleiku. Because our initial living space on the ship had been damaged, the kids and I needed to relocate. Walking around the open deck was like being a pat of butter skimming across a skillet, so we had to move quickly. Soon we were able to squeeze into a spot along a wall offering some relief from the relentless sunshine.

Seawater collected where one side of the ship slanted towards the sea, forming a large pool. Some used the flooded area to cool off; others used it to bathe. Both activities required being fully clothed, because one never knew what other passengers (or creatures) might be sharing the facilities. The sight of people strolling about the deck or gathered in groups around this crude pool contributed a surreal, almost luxury-cruise-like feel to our voyage, except that this "cruise" came without a buffet, cozy deckchairs and cool, umbrella-domed drinks.

It didn't take long for a few soldiers to identify me as a damsel in distress. Little did they know, this was not exactly true. Given my experience working in a male-dominated office, as well as my exposure to aggressive men while working for the political party in Pleiku, I knew how to handle myself. But in this harsh, dog-eat-dog environment, having some added protection certainly would not hurt. And these were young, chivalrous soldiers driven by duty and honor, not criminals; I welcomed their company.

The small group of enlisted men invited us to share their space towards the rear of the boat. Though uncovered, it was situated within a walkway between two structures, providing ample protection from the sun and room to lie down.

I was lucky and extremely grateful to find that while our situation seemed to bring out the worst in some people, there were other kind souls who banded together for strength and reached out to those in need. And thankfully, I didn't have to promise to marry all of them in exchange for their generosity. In some cases, though, it took some serious persuasion to obtain what was needed. One of my military "husbands-to-be" wielded some influence—and his service weapon— to acquire a ration of milk from another passenger for my daughter.

My biggest surprise while at sea was the reappearance of someone from my past—a beggar boy I'd met on my way home from a shopping trip during my first year in Pleiku. I say we met, but to put it more accurately, this boy presented himself to me, just as he did to many of the other shoppers in Pleiku's crowded marketplace.

He was maybe ten years old the first time I saw him. This poor urchin, as dirty and disheveled as the streets he prowled, would boldly confront people for handouts. If they refused, he would flash them his private parts. This was especially true if the mark was a woman.

I never knew his name, where he lived or if he had parents. But I knew his reputation long before I ever met him. Everyone advised me to avoid him, and I did my best to heed their warnings. I would cross to the other side of the street whenever I saw anyone who fit his description coming my way.

With such vigilance, it took a while before I made contact with the infamous "dirty little beggar boy" of Pleiku. But when we finally met—and then years later, when we again crossed paths on the oil tanker—I learned a valuable lesson about humanity and the enduring truth of the biblical verse, "Things that are despised, God has chosen."

For our second meeting, the boy was a teenager. His face had matured, but his eyes were the same ones I had tried to avoid many times before in the marketplace. They revealed the hardened gaze of someone who has, in such a short lifetime, witnessed the worst humanity has to offer. When I asked how he made it all the way to Saigon, he told me he had walked there by himself.

He might have walked right on by us, without doing or saying anything (just as I had done to him on the streets), but he noticed Mai lying limply in my lap and was drawn to her. He could tell she needed help. "Give me her bottle," he said. I only had one, and I had been guarding it closely. But for some reason, I trusted him enough to hand him the bottle.

He easily slipped through the crowds of people waiting for rations. Being that he was so grimy and pungent, most people gave him a wide berth. Upon discovering there was no milk available, he managed to get a double ration of rice juice to fill Mai's bottle.

Barefoot, filthy and in rags, this boy—this flasher I had once avoided—was truly an angel and the greatest example of a survivor I've ever known. Rather than becoming bitter or spiteful or simply giving up, he somehow changed his daily burden into a truly amazing ability to show compassion.

I promised myself I would try to never again judge people based on their outward appearance or supposed social standing. Appearances are often deceiving. True beauty is in the soul. The beggar boy taught me to appreciate and seek the beauty in everyone I meet.

I never thought to ask the boy for his name. I regret that now. If I could speak to him today, I would tell him he is beautiful, a true angel on earth, and I appreciate his selfless deeds. He helped my daughter when she needed it most, and I will never forget him.

The boy refilled Mai's bottle several times throughout our journey and regularly came back to check on her. With his help, she avoided dehydration, but she still was not receiving enough nourishment. She grew weaker each day and eventually got sick. With only one doctor on board to serve more than 1,000 people, it was a struggle to get any medical attention. To move up on the doctor's priority list, desperate passengers offered him bribes of money or whatever else they had.

A few days later, after what seemed like an eternity, the ship stopped in Manila, Philippines, for a maintenance check and to allow passengers to seek medical treatment. We made it just in time to get Mai the attention she needed. But I will always have great empathy for those who feel they have no choice but to compromise their bodies for the sake of their children.

As Mai's condition worsened, with no money to pay for what amounted to black-market medical care, I began to consider alternative "payment" methods. I knew that if it came down to it, I was prepared to give (or do) anything to save my children's lives.

In Manila, the ship was inspected to ensure its ability to continue on to our ultimate destination of Guam. We were docked alongside an American ship that had answered our crew's distress call. Relief workers boarded our leaning, leaky transport to provide whatever help they could. The injured and deceased were carried off. Food and supplies were carried on.

Mai finally got the fresh milk and medical attention she needed. I felt like I had not put her down since leaving my aunt's house three days earlier. Although Mai had probably lost a few pounds from dehydration, she was beginning to feel heavy. When I handed her to an American nurse for a check-up, my aching arms still hurt from carrying her but also longed to have her back. For the first time since Pleiku, I knew Mai and Bang were safe.

Our ship, though it still slumped to one side, was deemed seaworthy. The exaggerated tilt slowed our progress so much that it took another full week to reach Guam. The first thing we saw upon reaching port was a group of American journalists waiting to board. After a week at sea and sleeping under the stars (thank God we had no rain), the last thing any of us wanted to do upon arrival was delay, even for another minute, getting off that boat. But the Americans had to have their interviews, so they climbed aboard to authenticate their stories and attempt to convey to the world what it was like to be a "boat person."

Because I had already worked my way towards the exit to get ahead of the crowd, I happened to be one of the first people the reporters bumped into. A mother traveling alone with two young children under her arm, I really got their attention. I didn't know these were broadcast journalists. I didn't care anything about being on television anyway. I just wanted to ask for their help finding my half-sister, who lived in Norfolk, Virginia with her husband, Captain Ralph A. Smith.

There I was, in the worst condition of my life. And I was about to be unknowingly broadcast around the globe. I may not have been presentable or capable of putting together a single coherent sentence in English, but I could not pass up what might be my only opportunity to connect with family in the U.S. When the reporter began talking to me, I had no clue what he was asking. All I said in reply was something I had memorized while at sea: "I am looking for Navy Captain Ralph A. Smith." Along with another half-sister who lived somewhere in Maryland, Captain Smith and my half-sister in Norfolk were the only personal connections I knew of in America. So this was the only important thing I had to say at the time.

My message never reached Captain Smith or either of my half-sisters, but it did get the attention of some people with the International Rescue Committee (IRC) in Washington, D.C. Somehow this brief televised appearance helped expedite my journey to the U.S. a month later.

We were able to disembark when the journalists finally had their interviews. Bang, Mai and I were some of the first to descend the gangplank. Upon reaching the pier and finally setting foot on solid, level ground, I heard someone call my name. It was Lieutenant Hoe, who was still alone.

"Thuong, you need clothes. Please take these," he urged, presenting me with his wife's suitcase, which he had carried for the past ten days, along with his hope of finding her. He was giving up both. "I don't believe I'll have any use for it," he said. With that, he sat the tattered suitcase down next to me, gave my free hand a gentle pat to finalize the transaction and then was gone—as if pulled away by the undertow of the crowd—before I could utter the words "thank you," which stuck in my throat.

Hanging on to both of my children, a purse and now a suitcase, I fell in step with the throngs of people being directed by relief workers away from the ship and down a dirt road. Getting off the boat quickly had given me the advantage of slipping past most of the crowd. Before we reached the camp entrance, I wanted to put as much distance as I could between me and the amorous bodyguards to whom I had promised wedded bliss upon arrival.

To make better time, I knew I had to lighten my load. I paused to relieve myself of the hefty piece of shrapnel I'd acquired the day we left the Port of Saigon. The memory it sparked was probably best left behind anyway.

As we moved up the road—really more of a path—I was not sure where we were supposed to be going. But I knew I wanted to get there quickly. I had no sense of direction, because being just under five feet tall, I could not see beyond the dense hedgerow of refugees around me.

I occasionally looked around at the people who were my companions for this wretched parade, longing to find at least one familiar face. But these people were all strangers—their spirits broken and every face smeared with the same dust, fear and sorrow. No one spoke. We just trudged ahead, moving up the path like zombies. Despite these conditions, I was relieved to be off the ship and told myself it could only get better. After a mercifully short hike, we came to another swell of people moving through a long line of tents. All were new arrivals from various parts of Southeast Asia, waiting for clearance to enter the refugee camp set up by the U.S. military and international aid organizations.

As we were herded towards the gate, several lines began to form. While most people from our ship continued in one direction, I turned towards a different line and away from my cohorts—again attempting to throw the male harem I had collected off my scent.

Beyond the entrance were several more tents. Some were for general health checks and immunizations. Others were for completing admission forms and collecting census-type information, such as country of origin and number of family members.

On the admission forms, we were asked to rank our preferred destinations for relocation. Our options were sites in Texas, California and Florida. My two half-sisters lived in Virginia and Maryland, so I put down Florida as my first choice, thinking that was as near as I could get to either of them. Even though we weren't close, I thought they would be willing to help if they knew I was coming. I was wrong.

Once we completed the registration process, we crossed over to the main camp, where I was struck by the sight of a thousand tents— filthy umbrellas giving shade to a vast refugee wasteland. Walking through a seemingly endless grid of canvas, I somehow found our assigned tent—the primitive barracks we would share with about fifty others. With its rows upon rows of bare cots and earthen floor, the tent was reasonably clean and spacious enough to provide every adult with a bed. Those of us with small children were expected to share our cots with them.

Though crowded, the tent was a huge step up from the swaying steel deck of a sinking oil tanker. And its location was another silver lining. Situated in what was widely considered to be prime tent city real estate, we were just a few tents away from a medical station and the dining area—or what the military would call a mess tent. Covered latrines and showers were adjacent to our tent.

Not since Saigon did Mai, Bang and I have ready access to such luxuries as real food, clean water and a nurse. We also enjoyed another convenience I had never known before—disposable diapers. I counted every shower and diaper change as a blessing.

I was told the typical layover time for refugees in the tent city was three to four months. If we were going to be there that long, I would need to keep my mind occupied and establish something resembling a normal routine—if only to maintain my sanity.

Most of the refugees spent their time standing guard over their luggage and belongings. I didn't have any belongings to guard, only my kids. Looking out for them meant getting away from this place as soon as possible.

While awaiting admission into the camp, I learned there were volunteer jobs available to help process incoming refugees. The position, it was rumored, also came with some perks. Volunteers were given badges that allowed them to move freely throughout the camp and administrative tents. And by helping expedite the right person's discharge application, one could make a little money on the side. But the main reason these positions were so coveted was that volunteers' names got moved higher up the list for discharge, thus hastening their own relocation to the U.S.

I didn't relish the thought of spending four months in the tent city, so I immediately decided this was the job for me. The positions were only open to those who could speak English, because volunteers were often expected to serve as interpreters for incoming residents during registration. No problem. By faking my way through the job application with the little English I knew, much as I had while working for American intelligence in Pleiku, I was "hired" on the spot.

Whether we were to remain in camp for a few days or a few months, I knew it would be critical to find a few trustworthy people to look after Bang and Mai while I worked, went to the bathroom or waited in line for food. I had to make friends fast. Life in the tent city—just like I've found it to be everywhere I've lived since then—would have been impossible without reliable care for my children. Luckily, on the cot right next to mine was another single mother named Nghia, whose children were maybe nine and fourteen years old. Nghia empathized with me and generously offered to babysit each morning while I volunteered.

I also befriended a married couple traveling to Guam with one of their brothers. The husband was a highly trained heart surgeon, and the wife was a pharmacist. I met the family while waiting in line for food during one of my first few days there. They became three more of my angels, whose kindness I relied on for a variety of things throughout my stay, not the least of which was childcare.

Though we would lose touch after our experience in the tent city, I visited the husband and wife some time later, on a trip to middle-of-nowhere, Pennsylvania. Upon our happy reunion, the first thing we asked each other was, "Now that you're in America, what are you doing in your new life?"

The couple jubilantly responded, "We wash dishes!"

I, an unskilled mother of two, replied, "I'm a waitress!"

Despite being a diverse group of people, those of us in the tent city had one thing in common: as refugees, we would all have to start over when we arrived in America.

I didn't have the means to buy anything before I began volunteering and figured out how to make a little money by helping others more quickly navigate the admissions and discharge processes. The Vietnamese currency I carried was worthless. So just as I had done on the ship, I flirted—both as a defense mechanism and as a means of exchange. I became adept at keeping men at a distance—far enough they would not try anything funny, but not so far that they would be unwilling to help get what my children needed to survive.

One gentleman even found me a small sewing kit, which came in handy. Upon opening Lieutenant Hoe's suitcase, I discovered his wife had been much taller than I, so I had to alter her clothing to fit me. My seamstress skills were just good enough to salvage a few outfits for myself. The rest I gave to others in need.

Having made many friends who were now helping to protect my children and me, I no longer had to propose marriage to strangers. This freed me to pursue genuine companionship—another bit of "normalcy." There was one gentleman, in particular, whose company I valued above all others. He was a captain in the Vietnamese Navy, and he was very kind to us, as many others had been. With him, there was no aggression or ulterior motives.

Over the course of a few weeks, our friendship grew. I would not say it was a full-blown romance, but the Captain and I definitely made an emotional connection. From him I learned that no matter where you are or the difficulties you might face, a good human relationship can help you endure just about anything.

In the evenings, I frequently went to the Captain's "house" a few tents away, after arranging for someone to keep an eye on my sleeping kids. Far from having formal dates, we would talk, drink beer and share whatever "fancy" snack was available from the PX. We held hands every now and then, but nothing more. Our old-fashioned friendship was very comforting and a welcome escape from reality. Perhaps, it was also a way to delay thinking about the uncertainties of the future or planning for what was to come.

After six weeks in camp, my name came up on the waiting list. Bang, Mai and I were transferred to a hotel near the airport. For the next three days, we shared what seemed at the time to be the cleanest room on earth with my new friend Nghia and her children. From the boat, to the camp barracks, to the hotel, the quality of our lodging was slowly improving. I was encouraged to think what housing might be like once we reached America.

※

I had requested relocation to Florida. Instead, we landed in Fort Indiantown Gap, Pennsylvania—a rural U.S. Army post that had recently been converted to a short-term camp for Southeast Asian refugees. Although this camp was an improvement over the one we had just left, it began to feel like we could not get away from military housing.

Thankfully, in less than a week, we were headed to Washington, D.C. The bus ride from rural Pennsylvania through the Appalachian Mountains, around Baltimore, and into the nation's capital was my last chance to clear my head and prepare our plan for survival.

My first six years in the U.S. would be purely about keeping my head above water and, on occasion, about just keeping my head. In many ways, reaching America after almost two months on a boat or in a tent was a case of "out of the frying pan and into the fire." The sobering tent city experience in Guam was my only preparation for the transition to my new reality, which was starting over in America.

I was headed to the U.S. with two children under age four, with no money, no job prospects and no support system. I could speak and understand only limited English. I was alone, staggered by the destruction of my once-comfortable life in Vietnam and still trying to recover from the shock of everything my family had just been through.

Even though there were many things I didn't have—a husband, a home, any personal possessions, a formal education or even childcare—I had to stay focused on what I did have: two children relying on me for everything. They needed me to be a rock. And in the beginning, at least, I had serious doubts about whether I could even take care of myself. But that's the funny thing about children; they are constant reminders that we must survive. In fact, my children were the ultimate motivation for me to not just survive, but succeed.

PART II

AMERICA

Chapter 6: *From One Boogeyman to Another*

I was surprised to find that even in the middle of June, America could be a cold place. After sweating through the few clothes we had while in the steamy South Pacific, we were unprepared for the chilly nights in the hills of Pennsylvania. The abrupt climate change took a toll on Mai, who had not yet regained her full strength. In Indiantown Gap, she came down with an acute case of bronchitis and began coughing up blood on the bus trip to Washington, D.C.

After a four-hour ride, we entered our fourth new city in as many months. Outside the Greyhound's weathered steel doors was a completely foreign world, and I felt pathetically unprepared. The war was suddenly gone. The blurry nightmare experience from which I had recently been awakened but could only partially remember was over. As incredible as our journey had been so far, I could not shake the feeling that there was more shellshock to come. I still was not sure how to mentally brace myself for the new challenges I was sure to face. I was Twenty-three years old and felt like a child again—an impulsive runaway who had not thought through her decision. Everything was unfamiliar, terrifying, fascinating and exhilarating. But Bang and Mai needed a mother with a plan, an adult who knew where she was going and what she intended to do when she got there.

With a relieved hiss, the bus eased to a stop in front of an unremarkable downtown building. As I studied it through my window, I thought that given its size and location, the building could just as easily have been a drycleaner's.

It was already dark in the capital city. As I labored up the aisle, both kids in my weary arms, I struggled to keep a grip on the new Samsonite suitcase I had bought with tips I collected as a tent city interpreter. Bumping too many seat backs as I moved forward, I managed to get the three of us down the bus steps and out into D.C.'s early evening air.

There, waiting alone and holding up a small IRC Welcome! sign like a beacon, was Jeanne McDaniels, head of the International Refugee Committee's D.C. headquarters and our official agency sponsor. Unofficially, she was another unexpected angel who would help guide me through my earliest challenges in this country.

I didn't have to explain all the details of Mai's condition to Jeanne. She could see right away that my daughter had a fever and was laboring to breathe, so she drove us straight to Children's National Medical Center. Getting into our first American home would have to wait until Mai got the care she needed.

Once we made it to the hospital, I felt a great sense of comfort. I've always thought of hospitals—even those in Vietnam—as the ultimate place of security, where doctors and nurses become saviors performing everyday miracles. Jeanne took care of everything at the admissions desk, including the complex paperwork that came with obtaining emergency healthcare coverage for someone who'd only been in the country for a few days. After Jeanne explained our situation and filled out the required forms, Mai was admitted and given an initial examination by a pediatrician whose name I will never forget, Dr. Annette Ficker.

I listened to Dr. Ficker's words as she carefully detailed Mai's condition and presented her plan for treatment. Most of the words came to me as gibberish, but her tone was so calm and confident, her eyes so warm and reassuring. I could tell just by being in her presence that my daughter was in capable hands. Dr. Ficker and Jeanne explained that Mai would need to stay in the hospital for several more days to get the care she required.

As soon as Mai was settled in a room and sleeping soundly, Jeanne took me and Bang across town to our new apartment. If not for Dr. Ficker's gentle, reassuring manner and the amazing care she provided, this would have been unthinkable. I would not have been able to tolerate even a brief separation from Mai, much less several more days with her staying in the hospital.

✍

Today, Washington, D.C.'s 2901 Connecticut Avenue is an upscale condo. In 1975 the building, though beautiful outside, was an aging tenement in need of an overhaul. While awaiting its makeover, the property was on loan to the IRC to help house the swell of Southeast Asian refugees cascading into the capital city. The sparsely furnished apartments had long been neglected, but the tenants crammed inside could not afford to be picky. I was just glad it was not another army barracks.

We were assigned a third-floor efficiency unit. From the moment I crossed the threshold, it was evident we would be sharing the place with an army of cockroaches that maniacally patrolled most of the apartment's square footage day and night. The paint on the walls was cracked and curling near the ceiling, which might have given the casual, optimistic onlooker the false impression of weathered Corinthian columns supporting the floors above us. In some places, wood lathe and plaster were visible beneath the surface of its thin top coating.

Despite all this, I considered our new home a marked improvement over every other space we had inhabited since Saigon— including the crowded, petroleum-laced deck of the tanker; the primitive, dust-smothered tent city in Guam; and the cold, stark barracks of Indiantown Gap.

Oddly enough, our small apartment included a walk-in closet, which I converted into a separate sleeping area just big enough to fit the crib Jeanne had procured for Mai. In the living room, I arranged two single beds into a V configuration and covered them with a comforter, creating a makeshift couch. The "new" piece of furniture served a dual purpose; it was both a sofa and adjoining beds for Bang and me.

The apartment may have been a bit shabby but, as I had promised myself I would do with the people I met going forward, I resisted the urge to condemn it based on appearance. I chose, instead, to look at our latest living arrangement as a minor blessing. It was our own space and the safest place we had been in months.

꙳

For the next few days, I spent as much time with Mai as possible. Jeanne arranged for an IRC volunteer named Ginny—a tall, gorgeous Filipino—to take me to the hospital each morning. Ginny also showed me how to navigate the city using the bus system, mainly so I could get to the IRC office.

I brought Bang with me to the hospital once or twice but otherwise entrusted him to the care of kind strangers in my building. Once again finding myself in dire need of assistance, I was able to identify a few willing babysitters among my new neighbors. One was an older Vietnamese woman who took care of her own grandchildren during the day. She understood my situation and was happy to have Bang join her small brood. She was so happy, in fact, that she agreed to watch him for free.

Because most of the building's residents were also refugees, it was very much a communal village. Perhaps it was cultural or maybe purely circumstantial but, whatever the reason, the residents of 2901 Connecticut Avenue in those days supported and watched out for one another. Obvious maintenance issues and other flaws aside, the apartment community, if measured only by the affordable childcare resources available within its walls, was the ideal environment for the single working mother I was about to become.

I used to think I led a trouble-free family life in Vietnam, until it all ended abruptly. My worries were few and usually linked to the distant but occasional threats of war and, in the last few months I was there, an unfaithful spouse. After just one week in the U.S., I had already begun to understand the many different but no less oppressive, struggles that millions of people in this country face—including, but certainly not limited to, inadequate housing, childcare, healthcare and employment.

※

During my first week in D.C., I met Stephanie Cole, a senior editor with National Geographic Magazine. In addition to her full-time work, Stephanie was an active philanthropist who regularly made generous contributions to the IRC. She was not a volunteer, and there was really no reason for her to take any personal interest in me or any other refugee, except that she was a very giving person who felt compelled to intervene and provide support at a time when millions of needy families were pouring into her city. Stephanie found my family and quickly tucked us under her warm angel wing. It was in her nature to want to do more for people than just write tax-deductible checks. She gave more of herself than could ever have been expected. From day one, she cared for my family and eased our assimilation into American society.

I tried to practice speaking English whenever Americans were around, and because the staff at the IRC always heard me talking when I was at their office, everyone thought I spoke the language fluently. This assumption led them to also believe I could find my way around. In other words, my foolish pride and the illusion of self-sufficiency essentially kept us from getting assigned to a sponsor family and precluded me from receiving the job leads and language training I really needed. I was not assigned to any ESL (or "English as a Second Language") classes, and to avoid embarrassment, I never inquired about them. Instead, I got by with the basic words and phrases I knew, such as "hello," "goodbye," "good morning," "good evening," "I don't understand," "what did you say?" "what does that mean?" and so on.

I became a victim of my own success—success at faking it, that is. I had fallen under the radar of the IRC system designed to help families like mine. We were lucky that Stephanie and her family kept us from slipping completely through the cracks. They gave us their support without me having to ask for their help.

Looking back, this independence probably made my kids and me who we are today. Had we been placed with a sponsor, I may have gotten a college degree—maybe even a post-graduate degree—and perhaps enjoyed a quicker route to what other people call a successful life. But had it worked out that way, I believe my story—and my life— would not have been as interesting or rewarding. I might have missed out on the many valuable lessons I learned along the way and the experiences that helped me (and my children) become more resilient and resourceful. God bless those who were able to find sponsors when they got to this country. But I think the steeper climb challenged me and allowed me to better appreciate the plight of millions of other struggling families facing similar, and even worse, circumstances. And it certainly influenced my motives for giving back.

Though my independent nature helped shape my American experience, my friendship with Stephanie and her family was, perhaps, the biggest influence on the direction my life would take in this country. She and her husband Tim took my family in. But even more importantly, they showed my children and me the same respect they showed their own friends and family. Our refugee status didn't matter a bit. To them, we were simply people who needed a little help.

Stephanie reassured me, encouraged me and boosted my confidence when I needed it most. She let me know there was honor in working hard to support my family, no matter what kind of work I did. She told me that both she and her husband had also waited tables in college. She had a way of not only making me feel welcome, but also making me feel like what I did mattered, which was what I needed more than anything else at that time. I wanted to feel like a valued individual, not just a number, not just one of a million refugees.

Stephanie also taught me about the importance of networking and helped me begin building a foundation of social support. She worked for an internationally renowned magazine, and her husband was a high-ranking director with the World Bank's International Monetary Fund. This power couple introduced me to their friends and colleagues, including Liz and Ron Fennel, both World Bank directors, who were among my earliest friends and benefactors. And through them, I met Ann Marie Hicks, whose husband was also with the World Bank. These were all smart, hardworking, interesting people of great influence, and they took turns inviting my family over to their homes. I came to know them as my "World Bank family."

It was rare that I ever left a World Bank family member's home empty-handed. There seemed to be an endless clothing supply for them to donate whenever we visited. These hand-me-downs were high quality. Even the kids' clothes came from the finest stores. But it really didn't matter where the clothes came from or what they cost. These donations helped me stretch the few dollars I had, so they were invaluable. The brand names stitched on them were simply a bonus.

Yes, my family was poor, but we dressed very well. And that's no small thing. Maintaining a polished appearance, even in the hardest times (like my final days in Saigon), gave me a self-esteem boost that provided a valuable psychological edge. Looking my best showed everyone (including me) that I respected and could take care of myself—which I believed won me half the battle of getting through the day.

Stephanie left such an indelible impression on my life. Our friendship ended prematurely when she died of breast cancer in 1985. But in the ten years we had together, she cared for my children and me, treated me as an equal and inspired me to do and be more than I ever thought I could.

About a week after we arrived in D.C., once Mai had recuperated and we had all settled into our apartment, it was time to begin my job quest—a daunting but necessary task.

My qualifications were not ideal. I did not have a college degree; I had minimal office experience from my time working as a switchboard operator in Pleiku; and despite having masqueraded as an interpreter in Guam, I still spoke very little English. I was not delusional enough to think U.S. employers would be impressed by my meager work experience and lack of practical skills. My options, like those of most new immigrants looking for work, were severely limited. Regardless, it took me only a few days to secure my first job.

I was walking home from the market one afternoon, hugging grocery bags tightly against my chest and was only a few steps from my apartment building when I heard a voice call out. The unusual, somewhat-strained voice had come from below street level. I stopped and looked for its owner.

With my attention focused on Mai's health and all the things I needed to do, I had taken little interest in the scenery between home and my three main destinations: the hospital, grocery store and IRC office. It was only then that I noticed the tiny restaurant.

"Do you want a job?" asked the gruff voice. The words came at me in English but were steeped in an accent I could not quite place or understand.

Even with my limited English vocabulary, one vaguely discernible word—"job"—stopped me cold. I turned towards the voice and saw a man—age spotted, wrinkled and no taller than me in my platforms—bent over and slightly trembling beneath a plain white-and-blue sign. *He looks harmless,* I thought, glancing from him to the words scrawled above his head of thinning gray fuzz. I could not decipher the lettering, but a more fluent person would have been able to discern that the restaurant was called Arabian Nights.

In the time it took to descend the few steps to the landing where the shaky, old man stood, I had already decided to accept whatever job he offered. Once inside the restaurant, I learned he needed a waitress. I glanced around the dining room. There were a dozen or so tables punctuated with small amber-tinted votives, and a trace of garlic and *shawarma* lingered in the air from the previous night. Although the place looked like a dive from the street, on the inside, it was rather elegant—small scale but upscale, a spotless white-linen, cloth-napkin kind of place. The owner told me he had been the head chef at an embassy, so I assumed (correctly) that the food was as delicious as it smelled. This was the nicest restaurant I had ever been in.

Since the owner didn't speak English very well, he was not particularly insistent that his new waitress be able to chat up customers. He said he only cared whether I looked good, smiled big and could bring people the food they ordered in a timely manner. I thought, *How hard could it be to bring food to a table?*

The waitress position was currently filled by the owner's wife— a chunky, fifty-something Portuguese woman. She usually wore a long skirt and blouse, with a hostess's apron to complete the dowdy ensemble. Her height and girth matched her husband's, but somehow she appeared taller—either because of her high heels, teased hair or maybe both. While she served as hostess, I would be the tiny restaurant's only waitress. I would also be its only staff member who was not family.

The owner's brother-in-law served as the cook. With dark hair and a face perpetually reddened from long hours up close to the grill, his appearance struck me as a little menacing. His wife—a plain, slender woman—washed dishes and assisted him in preparing some of the food, including the dressing that made the house salad one of the restaurant's signature offerings.

My first few days at Arabian Nights were like the first days in a new elementary school. I was afraid to do anything wrong. But wrong or right, I constantly felt like I was being kept in line. I flashed back to reciting multiplication tables in my grandmother's kitchen, only this time my taskmaster was the restaurant owner's wife. She was very critical; at least, I sensed this from her tone. I could not understand most of her English-Portuguese fusion. Luckily, there was one language we shared, and when she needed to give me important instructions, she resorted to French. "*Plus vite, plus vite!"* (meaning "Faster, faster!") was one of her favorite commands.

Once a sheltered Vietnamese woman, I was now struggling as a waitress-in-training. The experience was all new to me. The wife had worked in restaurants since she was a young girl and was now trying to impart a lifetime's worth of knowledge to me in short order. She worked very quickly and efficiently, so I had to work even harder just to keep up.

My main responsibilities early on were delivering the food and bussing tables. The wife tried to teach me how to hoist full trays—which seemed to be the size of small canoes—over my head and balance them on one hand. This was a feat her wider, sturdier frame could accommodate. Not mine. I had to carry the trays like loads of laundry, with arms outstretched and the weight supported by my midsection. This made it challenging to pass through doorways and between tables.

I shadowed the wife for the first two weeks while she did most of the waiting on and conversing with customers. All our tips were stuffed into a can until the end of my shift, when she would carefully count out twenty dollars and hand it to me like a mother giving an allowance to her child. She pocketed the rest. Each day she gave me the same amount, regardless of the actual tips I earned, which was often $100 or more. Since I was only getting paid $1.19 per hour, twenty dollars still seemed generous. For those two weeks, I went home exhausted. And the daily cash tips were a little salve for my aching feet and limbs.

By closely watching the wife's every move, imitating her mannerisms and quickly memorizing every menu item by its corresponding number, I was soon able to take over more waitressing duties. Getting the number system down was critical to my success, as the cook seemed to understand the customer orders I barked into the kitchen better when I used numbers than when I pronounced the words in my accent. The process actually reminded me of the coded messages I'd delivered in my radio operator's job in Pleiku. I was surprised to learn that I did, indeed, have some professional skills that transferred!

Even after I took on full responsibility for serving customers, the owner's wife continued to ration my tips. And whenever I walked from the kitchen to the dining room, the owner would meet me in the narrow doorway and take the opportunity to push his grotesque body against me. I was helpless with my arms full of serving tray and dishes. Occasionally, he would paw at my behind as he squeezed past. It was horrible and disgusting, not to mention uncomfortable. But I needed the job to provide for my children. In Vietnam, twenty dollars a day plus an hourly wage was a fortune, and for a desperate immigrant with a family to feed, it was still pretty good money. So I just did my best to avoid him and ignore his improper behavior.

One of the fringe benefits of working at Arabian Nights was the opportunity to meet an eclectic mix of customers. Most of them were very sophisticated, affluent and generous tippers, not that it mattered to a waitress getting a flat share of the daily take.

One regular customer—a sixty-year-old, wealthy Jewish gentleman named Albert Brick—didn't just come for the meals. As I would later learn, he actually came to visit me. Mr. Brick also served as the owner's legal counsel, which I initially assumed was why he ate at the restaurant so frequently. But the more I saw of Mr. Brick, the more he took an interest in my background as a refugee, always asking me how I was doing and whether my children were okay.

The first two pieces of advice Mr. Brick ever gave me, I thought were interesting: "Learn a trade and be sure to marry rich." He encouraged me to be more entrepreneurial and follow my instincts. One day Mr. Brick gave me his business card and told me to come see him if I ever needed anything.

One day I would. But for the time being, I had Arabian Nights—which, despite all its imperfections, also offered me intangible benefits like a friendship with Mr. Brick. I was thankful to have my first job in America.

Chapter 7: *Running to Stand Still*

To supplement my small, unsteady income, I found two roommates. Like me, they were both waitresses who needed a break. Unlike me, they were runway models—tall and sexy. One was separated from her abusive American husband. She had gone to the IRC for help but, because she was married to an American citizen, they would not sponsor her. I met her at the IRC office, learned of her plight and promptly took her in. Our third roommate was her co-worker.

The pair of them floated from one job (and party) to another. In Vietnam, they would likely have been labeled "bar girls," which was considered better than being a prostitute. But they didn't seem much different from me. They were just two helpless young ladies set adrift in Washington D.C., doing what they could to make ends meet and find some joy in life.

Our rent was covered by the IRC, so I used the little cash my roommates gave me to help pay for food. With their contributions, my financial situation only marginally improved. Then it dramatically worsened when my reliable pro-bono babysitter moved and I had to scramble to find another.

The stressful hunt for affordable childcare would become one of the biggest struggles in my life. Fortunately, with so many other immigrant families in my building, it was not difficult to quickly find a replacement. However, while the family I found to care for Bang and Mai asked for reasonable compensation, they would not do it for free. My waitressing salary was enough to buy groceries, clothes, diapers and other necessities, but it would not cover a full-time babysitter. Thus began the search for job number two.

After a few weeks of regularly visiting the IRC office to report progress and fill out paperwork, I developed a rapport with one of the English-speaking Vietnamese secretaries. I told her I was interested in finding office work and asked her to keep me in mind should she come across any opportunities.

The first position she found for me was working as a reel-to-reel tape threader in a small M Street office in Georgetown. I didn't know what reel-to-reel tape was, how it was used or why anyone would need to have it threaded. But compared with waiting tables, this more closely resembled what I considered a "real" job. It was in an office and paid top dollar: $3.15 an hour. I asked the secretary, "Can I start today?"

The work was monotonous, of course. For eight hours a day, I took giant reels of tape and made them into smaller ones. But for nearly three times what I earned at the restaurant, boredom was a small price to pay.

Waitress. Tape threader. Neither of those titles evoked adventure, glamour or even so much as a hint of the word "career" in my mind. My next job opportunity, introduced to me by a Vietnamese friend, had at least the first two elements.

When my friend told me about the job, he called it an "underground casino," which I took to mean a casino on the lower level of a building, like the restaurant where I worked, which was below street level. When it came to jobs, I was open-minded. I agreed to go with him to meet the casino's owner one evening after work.

The casino was located in the damp basement of some nondescript building on H Street in the heart of D.C.'s Chinatown. As many warning bells as this should have set off for me, I didn't yet know enough to be afraid. We drove into an alley and entered the building through a side door. There was no doorman and no signage to indicate anyone ever used this entrance except to take out the garbage from the Chinese restaurant above.

On the other side of the unmarked door was a short stairway, leading to an even shorter hallway, which led to yet another unmarked door. Beyond it was a dimly lit, fifteen-square-foot room that once may have been the basement of an old townhouse. This, I was disappointed to learn, was the "casino."

The gambling parlor's all-male occupants were further obscured by billowing clouds of cigar and cigarette exhaust. The walls and cement floor were completely bare. Three felt-topped Pai Gow tables stood along the walls, facing the center of the room. Gamblers, six to a game, hugged the padded table edges while another dozen spectators hovered around them, eagerly awaiting the first vacant seat. All of them smoked heavily while they focused their bloodshot eyes on the movement of the chattering black tiles.

It took a minute for the owner to spot the young female who had just entered his lair through the haze. The rest of the crowd barely noticed us as they continued to expel smoke with every bet and tile placed. The interview lasted as long as it took for the pit boss to look me up and down. I was a young woman. I was hired—seven dollars an hour, no experience necessary.

The job fit perfectly into my schedule, because I would only have to work weekends. I started the next Friday night working the graveyard shift from midnight to 7:00 a.m.

I had grown accustomed to not understanding much of what was happening around me since I had come to America. Chinese Pai Gow was no different. As a dealer's apprentice, my job was to stand next to him and watch the controlled chaos unfold. The only woman in the room, I was strategic window dressing, giving the place its only real pizzazz and serving as a distraction to give the house an added advantage.

If players at my table won, they would give me a small tip and say,

"Hey, you sure are lucky!" It felt strangely uplifting to be reminded, even by some strange gambler in the seedy bowels of Chinatown at 3:00 a.m., just how lucky I really was. While my family and so many other unfortunate people were still trapped in Vietnam, I was here, safe from the war, with two healthy kids, living and working freely.

Tips were my only indication whether people were winning or losing, because the game made no sense to me. More or less, it was honor among thieves—thieves who sent me home the first night with an extra thirty dollars in cash. That money, I thought, was not only going to feed my children; it would also get me closer to bringing my family to America.

Now holding down three jobs, I began my days by dropping Bang and Mai off at the neighbor's apartment at 7:30 a.m., then taking a bus to Georgetown, where I threaded tape until 4:00 p.m., when I rushed to catch another bus, which got me to the restaurant by four-thirty. Those bus trips were the only time I had to myself in those early days. I often spent this time thinking about my family, wondering where they might be, and promising myself that, as soon as I could, I would let them know we were okay and that I was working to get them out. It was a promise I would keep, but not for several more years.

For a few weeks, I would leave the restaurant on Friday nights at around 11:00 p.m. to go home, change clothes and check on Bang and Mai. My roommates had moved out and my half-brother Hâu had moved in, so he watched the kids while I worked nights. Hâu had been a physics professor in Vietnam. After failing to find a teaching job when he arrived in America shortly before I did, he had settled on a dishwashing position at a small restaurant in the city.

At around 11:30 p.m., I would find a ride from one friend or another into Chinatown, where I would work until the next morning. For better or worse, this tight schedule didn't last. A couple of weeks later, I was unable to make it to work. I don't remember why, but it turned out to be another instance of everything happening for a reason. That night the casino was raided by police and everyone was arrested. Just like that, my stint as a

Pai-Gow-dealing enchantress was over.

Yes, I was lucky—probably more than I know. Jail and a fine might not have been the only punishments I avoided that night. During my short time working there, I got the sense that the hostess-dealer position was only a gateway to another, darker existence filled with unsavory tasks. On more than one occasion, I thought I caught the pit boss glancing at me with a nod and smirk that said, "You're an asset to me now. Soon you'll be worth even more."

A few weeks after the casino raid, I quit my tape-threading job. I had been there for almost two months and still was not sure if I was performing the task correctly most of the time. This translated into me doing the job poorly and drawing the ire of my supervisor. The meager wage I was bringing home after taxes was not worth the stress of constantly being scolded. Two jobs down, one to go.

It was the cook, not my boss, who ended my days at Arabian Nights. Years before, I'd been hired by a political party in Pleiku. I was young and one of very few Vietnamese women present in male-dominated political circles. My job was to help coordinate and attend fundraisers and other social events, which I embraced as a great excuse to dress up and get out of the house. The events were also dominated by men, so I dealt with aggressive, often inappropriate, behavior from them frequently. I had heard all the lines and seen every move. At times I was flattered by the attention, but that's as far as it went.

These artful skills of deflecting male aggression helped save me countless times throughout my life, but they almost failed me one day at the restaurant. It was the first time I could remember feeling I was in danger with a man in the U.S.

One Monday, the cook told me he needed to talk to me alone the next day. He said the owner had mentioned something to him about me, and he wanted to discuss it with me. Since the restaurant was closed on Tuesdays, there would be no one around, and we could talk in private.

I thought he was going to tell me that his brother-in-law was unhappy with my work and then fire me. I felt mildly panicked for the rest of my shift. I could not stop thinking, I can't lose this job; it's the only one I have left!

The next morning at around 11:00 a.m., I entered the restaurant. I was anxious to hear what the cook had to tell me, but something made me feel uneasy and told me I probably shouldn't be in the empty restaurant alone. Hearing the front door close, the cook came out from the back, looking nervous. He locked the door behind me and said we should talk in the kitchen, where he felt more comfortable (it was basically his office). Somehow, this made sense to me. I was more afraid of being fired than anything else. I had no reason to suspect what would happen next.

As soon as the kitchen doors swung closed behind us, he was on me. He pushed me down onto the food prep table. As its metallic top cut into my shoulder blades, losing my job was the furthest thing from my mind. I knew I was in trouble.

Lying there on my back, I looked up at all the knives, pots, pans and other kitchen utensils hanging over my head—sharp things, heavy things, serrated things, things that could be used as weapons. Maybe by me, but probably by him. I was sure if I didn't give in, he would kill me. Then he would chop or grind up my body so no one would ever find me. My options were severely limited: relent or try to grab a weapon.

He was too big for me to break free and have a chance at one of the implements dangling above me. Instead, my weapon of choice was one that served me well on the journey from Saigon to Guam. With the breath I had left after my assailant's sudden and violent advance, I summoned my most flirtatious voice from deep within. In just a few words I knew he would understand, I told him it would be better for us to go somewhere else to "do it"—somewhere "more comfortable," like my apartment. But first he would have to let me up.

He tried to kiss me. I dodged his advance, slipped off the table and got around to the other side of him so that I had my back to the kitchen entrance. "Wait, not here," I repeated, slowly trying to remove the quiver from my voice. "Table no good ... next door ... come with me." By some miracle, he fell for it. He let me up with a sickening smile on his face.

Straining to return the smile and pretending I was still interested, I shuffled towards the door. If only I could reach the relative safety of the dining room and its big windows, I might have a chance to show someone what was happening to me.

Once I made it to the dining room, the restaurant's front door still seemed 100 yards away. My feet felt heavy, my head light. I tried not to show him any sign of my panic as I clumsily turned the deadbolt, looking back for one last tentative smile before pulling myself through the door. Once outside, I hit the stairs running so fast that I came right out of my platforms. My bare feet hit the sidewalk, and I was in a dead run before he knew what was happening.

I didn't look back to see if he was chasing me. I ran in the opposite direction from my building and around the block, hoping he would be unable to follow me home, not slowing down until I collapsed inside my apartment. I never went back and never told anyone why I left—not the police, not my family, not anyone at the IRC, not even Mr. Brick. I was angry and ashamed—angry at the cook for attacking me and taking away my only means of supporting my kids and ashamed for foolishly putting myself in such a risky position.

I knew I could not dwell on any of it. I had to keep moving forward, and that meant pushing the whole terrible incident down deep inside— deep enough that no one else could see how vulnerable I really was. I needed work, not sympathy. To impress prospective employers, I would need to present a confident exterior, no matter how much I was trembling inside. I told myself, Nobody wants to hear about how needy and broken you are or how bad your life has been up to now. They, just like your children, want to know that they can count on you to do your job today and tomorrow and the next day.

After four months of working six and sometimes seven days a week, I was now completely unemployed. The next morning, I woke up early, dressed and fed my kids, put on my best outfit, makeup and heels and headed to the IRC office to start over again.

Like sinking into quicksand, the harder I struggled to get up and out, the further down I went. I was basically looking for work so that I could afford rent, food and childcare ... so that I could keep working. I needed a new strategy. Maybe Mr. Brick was right, I thought. Maybe the only way to earn enough to support my kids (and actually get time off to see them) would be to learn a trade.

My escape from Arabian Nights had erased most, but not all, of my naïveté and taught me several early lessons about what to expect while struggling to survive as a young, single mother and immigrant in a big city. One was that some people, no matter how friendly and honest they seem, will take advantage of you if you let them. Amazingly, it took a few more years before my guard was fully up and I had developed a healthy skepticism about the motives of helpful strangers.

Meanwhile, there was still a good amount of wide-eyed optimism and blind trust left in me. After all, I was only in my early twenties, practically still a kid myself. Because I had urgent needs and big plans for every cent I could take in, I remained open to any and all employment opportunities— even if those propositions came from chance meetings on the street.

While I waited for job leads from the IRC, I had people approaching me on the streets of D.C. all the time, offering me a variety of short-term opportunities, most of them unsavory. Even the few short-term positions I pursued weren't exactly helping me build the career I would need to sustain my family long term.

A week after I fled the restaurant, a young man stopped me on the sidewalk and asked, "Do you want to be my model?" He said he was a photographer building a portfolio of his work. The idea intrigued me, given my "extensive modeling experience" with the war photographer in Kon Tum. I was excited to relive that wonderful, dreamlike afternoon and that feeling of freedom. It didn't matter that most models were much taller than me, or that the guy suggested we meet at my apartment instead of an actual studio. By the time I heard those little details, I was already hooked by the fantasy and the ten dollars an hour he promised. I thought, *Wow, my hourly wage just skyrocketed!*

I was so excited about my big break in the modeling business that I bought a cheap, long gown to wear for my first sitting. The next day, when the budding photographer arrived at my home, he explained that I was to be shot in a variety of lovely lingerie. For some reason, I was fine with this. He was very polite and professional about it. And for the next two hours, I posed like a Victoria's Secret vixen. Maybe he really was building his portfolio; maybe he wanted to date me. I don't know, but it was an easy twenty dollars, and technically I was clothed.

Shortly thereafter, another freelance photographer approached me on my way home. "You have this certain impish look in your eyes that I'd love to capture on film," he told me.

When he offered me twenty dollars an hour to be photographed wearing a wide selection of formalwear and lingerie, I was all ears. Like the first freelancer, he was an older man, maybe in his fifties. But this one was married. When he arrived at my apartment for our photo session, he brought an album overflowing with pictures he had taken of his wife—nude, but tasteful. One especially artistic shot showed her bare torso in the shape of a cello, taken from behind as she knelt.

I'm not sure if it was because I could not recreate the impish look on cue or that I was much shorter than the average model, but my career in front of the camera died after just two sittings. *Does "impish" mean naked?* I wondered.

⁓

In addition to frequent advice and monetary gifts, Mr. Brick provided me with the occasional money-making opportunity. Convinced I had a future in sales, he once introduced me to a friend who needed salespeople for a door-to-door lingerie business (which was as crazy as it sounds). *I've got experience in that area!* I thought.

After adequately demonstrating my limited knowledge of and skill for modeling intimate apparel to Mr. Brick's friend, I was given a startup inventory of corsets, nighties and thongs. I was to sell these items, starting at my own apartment complex. In a community of poor immigrants, however, lingerie was mildly appealing but not exactly in high demand—not even to one of the more affluent residents, a famous Vietnamese singer who lived down the hall.

When I told Mr. Brick I had not sold a thing, he said, "My friend says if any of it fits, it's yours." I was sure he was just trying to make me feel better and that he had paid for it all himself. I didn't have a job or own any attire that could be considered professional, but I was set for life with lingerie.

⁓

I soon landed a real sales job. I secured a retail position at the Sheraton Washington Hotel gift shop, which was just a few minutes' walk from my apartment building. It only paid $3.50 per hour (a fraction of what I assumed top models were earning), but it was steady money. And in such a nice hotel. I got to dress up and wear high heels every day, which I considered a fun perk.

I was given plenty of responsibility for the success of the shop, including managing inventory and customer relations. This fed my entrepreneurial spirit. And meeting the shop's manager—an attractive, impeccably-dressed woman—also inspired me. I thought, *I'm finally making real progress towards my goal of being a professional business woman. I can do this.* Looking like a professional had me beginning to feel like one too. But as much as I was learning on the job, the pay was still low, and the hours standing in high heels were long. I knew it was not going to be a long-term solution.

After two months at the Sheraton, with Mr. Brick's words about learning a trade ringing in my ears, I went to the IRC to ask for help identifying and enrolling in some kind of training program. By this time I had met so many people through my work at the restaurant and gift shop that my English was improving just through conversations with customers and friends like Mr. Brick and Stephanie. Little by little, I was getting better at communicating. I felt more comfortable. I felt ready for the challenge of a classroom.

The IRC recommended I enroll in La Cave Academy, an institution offering a wide range of professional training. It was a place where many other immigrants had been directed before me and had experienced varying degrees of success. Even though tuition would be free, thanks to a refugee grant, I was taking another leap of faith. I was embarking on an actual career path. I was going to be … a secretary.

Chapter 8: *Flight of the Bumblebee*

One thing I wish I had known before enrolling in secretarial school is that writing in shorthand is an extremely hard thing to do. In fact, I knew next to nothing about what secretaries did, except that they worked in offices, usually for big shots, earned steady pay and got to sit in comfortable chairs. Those all were things I could handle and being a secretary had to be better than waitressing. I was sold on the idea—but not the least bit prepared for what I was getting into.

La Cave Academy, an institution that sent its graduates out into the world as bartenders, executive secretaries, restaurateurs and aspiring hotel magnates, was located downtown on 14th Street. This area was notorious in those days for being a burgeoning sex-and-drug corridor. Each day I walked the few blocks from the bus stop on K Street, down 14th, past a gauntlet of working girls, drug dealers and sex shops—all openly displaying their elicit wares. When friends asked how I was doing, I told them, "Very good. I'm going to school on 14th Street." It sometimes took a moment to remember I should qualify my answer by adding, "It isn't what you think!"

Of course, I did have to turn down more than my share of propositions each day: "Hey, Miss … twenty dollars … sleep with you?" In that neighborhood, this kind of thing probably would have happened regardless of my penchant for wearing mini dresses, high heels and liberal amounts of eye makeup. The more I tried to look good, the more attention I got. Sometimes it was the wrong kind of attention.

My daily commute to La Cave's four-story brick building was not so intimidating during the bright daylight hours. Leaving the school at night was another story. Even under a dusky streetlamp haze, the walk required a higher level of vigilance. I tried not to judge these people. In fact, when I occasionally caught the eye of one of the destitute—particularly the young ones who haunted those littered sidewalks and shadowy alleyways—I found myself wondering where their parents were and what tragedies had placed these sons and daughters into these circumstances. I tried to empathize with them, which was not too hard since I was in my own struggle to survive while supporting my two children.

In my daily comings and goings from La Cave, I could not help but be reminded of the beggar boy from Pleiku. And every time I walked through the school's doors, I felt immense pressure, knowing what could happen if I didn't succeed inside this building—this oasis of education and potential in a neighborhood bound by squalor. I had to do more than make my best effort; I had to achieve something. If I failed, there was a very real possibility I could join the procession of those suffering on the streets outside.

La Cave was my best chance so far to avoid that brutal cycle of poverty. But it didn't take long for me to identify the one stumbling block in my path to a better life for my kids and me. My "single bad break"—my nemesis—was Introduction to Shorthand.

Before entering La Cave, I had been able to fake my way in and out of several jobs and other sticky situations by making the best of my scant English abilities. For non-native speakers like me, already struggling to read and write English in "long hand," the shorthand version was impossible. But until I mastered this vital skill, getting a job as an executive assistant would also be impossible. Too bad I didn't know this important information when I registered for classes. If I had realized the odds of me becoming an executive secretary were only slightly better than me becoming a Buddhist nun, I might have chosen a different course of study and saved myself a lot of grief. But I still gave it my best shot—twice.

I had falsely assumed that this "short" version of English would make it quicker and easier to learn. Silly me. Copying and memorization served me well while learning to type but could only get me so far with shorthand. While I could identify individual words by matching them with the French vocabulary I knew and could memorize the multitude of shorthand symbols to which they corresponded, translating those symbols back into polished English required a much better command of the language than I possessed.

Technically, I completed Introduction to Shorthand. I attended every class and attempted all the exercises. But it was not a class where they gave out passing grades for memorizing new vocabulary or for simply trying your best. You either got it all (and got it right) or you didn't.

I didn't just fail the class; I felt as though I had failed myself and my kids.

A friend once told me I reminded her of a bumblebee and, for a while, I was not sure why. I have always kept busy, but I don't consider myself more productive than anyone else, nor do I believe I am particularly graceful or agile like a bee.

I recently discovered something about bumblebees. Apparently there is a myth that says it shouldn't be possible for them to fly. The laws of aerodynamics seem to prove bees don't have the capacity to achieve flight, given their allegedly inadequate wing size and beats per second. One of the earliest potential sources for the myth is a reference in French entomologist Antoine Magnan's 1934 book *Le vol des insectes*. By applying what scientists knew about air resistance to insects, he found their flight to be unfeasible, in theory. Magnan explains in his introduction:

> *It is believed that the calculations which purported to show that bumblebees cannot fly are based upon a simplified linear treatment of oscillating aerofoils. The method assumes small amplitude oscillations without flow separation. This ignores the effect of dynamic stall, an airflow separation inducing a large vortex above the wing, which briefly produces several times the lift of the aerofoil in regular flight. More sophisticated aerodynamic analysis shows that the bumblebee can fly because its wings encounter dynamic stall in every oscillation cycle.*

With everything, including gravity, seeming to work against it, the bumblebee succeeds by doing a little bit more. The bumblebee's ability to fly is a miracle of nature—one that defies all odds, logic and laws of science. I now believe this is what my friend could have meant when she made her observation. I love that.

At this time in my life, I would need to invoke every bit of the resilient, odds-defying bumblebee spirit within me if I was going to move forward—not just with my career, but with something just as intimidating: my love life.

In addition to being a temporary source of income and questionable influence on my language skills, my roommates also helped expand my social circle. Being beautiful and outgoing, they never had any trouble finding men to take them out dancing or to the bars. While on the oil tanker and in the tent city, it seemed as though I was the girl many young soldiers were after (which, no doubt, had its positive and negative aspects). Now, in the U.S., the two beauties to whom I had given shelter got all the attention. Maybe I should have been a little jealous but, after my recent adventures in the restaurant industry, I was more than happy to have them attract most of the attention.

The girls were regulars on the club scene and often went out with the same group of Asian male friends. I was usually invited to join them but rarely had the luxuries of time, money, and a babysitter needed to enjoy a night of partying. I mostly got to know these men when they came to our apartment to pick up my roommates.

For my first opportunity to go out and meet potential dates, I was paired up with one of the roommates' friends. I'll call him Bachelor Number One. He was handsome enough but not a gentleman. Like the many other chauvinistic men who had made bold passes at me on the street, he could be disrespectful and relentless in his attempts to get whatever he desired—even from women he had just met. My roommates were more "experienced" with men. Because I lived with them, Bachelor Number One assumed I was easy to seduce. He was unpleasantly surprised to learn he was wrong.

A friend of mine named Thông became Bachelor Number Two. Thông lived in a building across the street from my apartment, and I would often see him while walking to the grocery store. He was also a Vietnamese refugee, so one day I introduced myself. I learned that Thông had once been an interpreter for the U.S. military and, like many who fled after the war, he had once made a very good living. Yet in this country, the best job he could find was working as a mechanic at a Volvo dealership. He was a kind man, but his perceived fall in social standing damaged his pride and made him a very sad person deep down. On nights when he stayed home alone, he drank as a way to forget.

Since I was also working at a menial job and struggling to make ends meet after fleeing the war, I think Thông saw me as a kindred spirit. Both our egos had taken hits and both of us were here alone. To ease the pain of his own loneliness, he began devoting all his time and energy to me. He thought he was easing my pain but, in truth, I was not lonely or hurting. I didn't have time for either emotion. I felt more fatigued and discouraged. I was tired from working all day and night and having little to show for it. I had no true direction and was not optimistic about my ability to extract my children from our current living conditions.

I didn't see myself becoming romantic with Thông. His was not the kind of energy that would propel me forward—though to be honest, his intense kindness nourished me in the short term. He made me feel appreciated and desired. Until meeting Thông, I had spent several months feeling like my personal needs were secondary to those of my children and of my family back in Vietnam. Working long hours and then going home to a rundown apartment and sleeping children who were deprived of their mother's attention had worn down my body and spirit. I knew this was not the way our lives were supposed to be. But until I had enough money to change everything, my needs were unimportant. My sole purpose was to work and serve the needs of my children.

With Thông, I had someone who showed interest in me— someone who asked me what I needed and wanted to see me all the time. His attention was flattering and a boost to my self-esteem. Whenever he was around, I felt special again. But I knew he didn't love me. I had learned to recognize the difference between love and infatuation … or pity. I knew what Thông had to offer me was fleeting. His sadness wore me down at a time when I needed all my strength.

Bachelor Number One came back into the picture long enough to introduce me to a polite friend of his named Chuong.

Chuong was from Saigon. He was very bright, spoke English and French fluently, and had been somewhat of a big shot back home. In Vietnam he had been a vice president for one of the country's largest corporations. In the U.S., he worked for an insurance company based in New Jersey, which is where he spent his weekdays. He came home to Virginia only on the weekends.

Chuong and I got to know each other well over the course of a few months. His commuting to and from New Jersey forced our friendship to develop gradually, which was more comfortable for me anyway. Since he was absent most of the week, he became extremely attentive when he was around, always going out of his way to do things for my children and me. Without being asked, he often brought us milk and other food, which helped me save on groceries. He ran all kinds of errands for me and gave me rides on the weekends, day or night, which saved me on bus fare.

Forever at my beck and call, Chuong was becoming an indispensable friend. To anyone else it would have been evident he wanted to date me, but I was oblivious to his romantic angling. I truly believed he felt sorry for my children and me, and I saw him as a caring brother I never had. He told me I was pretty. My real brothers told me I was ugly and that no one would ever love me. With my mind firmly locked on meeting the daily demands of supporting my family, it was no wonder my relationships with men were always out of kilter.

My ignorance about Chuong's true feelings was also due, in part, to his traditional Vietnamese passive-aggressive approach to romance. While I occasionally dated other people, Chuong sat patiently on the sidelines, always available to me and quick to dispense friendly guidance. Then, at the right moment, he would make strategic attempts to expose the missteps and character flaws of my potential suitors. Chuong tried to prove, in subtle ways, his superior candidacy. He was in a war of attrition with every other man who crossed my path. If he could not persuade me against his competitors, then he would simply outlast them.

As our friendship grew, Chuong took more liberties in sharing his opinions about how to take care of Bang and Mai, with whom I should socialize, where I should work, and even where I should live. He convinced me to move out of the city, which he believed was a dangerous place for me and a poor environment for raising children. I agreed. The timing was also right to make a move. I had just finished the semester at La Cave and was not going to return. This was an opportunity to put my failure there behind me, both mentally and physically.

Chuong also encouraged me to enroll at Northern Virginia Community

College (NOVA) to take the English classes I would need in order to excel in a trade school. Meanwhile, I could apply for federal welfare and find more affordable housing near him. All these things made the move more attractive to me. To Chuong, the most important thing was getting us closer to him—which addressed not only his concerns about my safety, but also my dating life.

In the late winter of 1976, with a distinct feeling of dé-jà vu, I went apartment shopping with Chuong in the Virginia suburbs, just as I had done with Binh on my first day in Pleiku. With all the upheaval that had transpired in the intervening years, I had become oblivious to the passage of time. It was hard to believe I had only been in the U.S. for nine months. And it felt much longer than five years since I had left my parents' home in Da Lat, still a child in many ways. Now Chuong was promising to help me find a similar haven in which to raise and protect my own children.

From the beginning, ours was an unusual relationship. Chuong wanted to be my hero. He wanted to rescue me. And after being taken advantage of—in one way or another—by most of the men I had met in America, losing three jobs, and stumbling through my first attempt at school in this country, I let him. He went about his courtship in true Vietnamese fashion—slow and stealthy. At the outset, Chuong made it his mission to make my life easier. And in his efforts to achieve this goal, he inserted himself into every area of it.

While I had some idea what I needed to do with my life, I didn't know how to get there. I didn't know what was even possible or what resources, outside of the IRC, an immigrant single mother had at her disposal. This was a time when I most needed someone who cared about my children and me—someone who had already transitioned from Vietnam and had established himself in America. In other words, I needed someone like Chuong.

Moving out of the city to an apartment close to him was, he assured me, the first step to solving my problems. Enrolling at NOVA would take care of my lingering difficulties with learning English and remove my final barrier to completing secretarial school. And the key to success, he promised, would be applying for welfare to cover expenses while I was in school.

We found a two-bedroom garden apartment on Donnybrook Court in the Virginia suburb of Annandale. It was just around the block from Chuong's apartment complex, so rather than driving all the way into D.C. with a McDonald's hamburger, fries and milkshake to satisfy my late-night cravings, he could be at my doorstep in less than ten minutes. Now I could truly enjoy fast food.

After I had settled into my new apartment, Chuong took me to the welfare office. Having handled applications for his elderly parents, he knew the system and how to get me through the process. Before this, I did not know the system even existed or that I could even ask for such help. But Chuong assured me that, for a single mother and recent immigrant trying to gain a foothold in this country, this was the right thing to do. He said it would just be until I was able to earn a steady paycheck again. Welfare was a safety net available to me only in America, and soon I was grateful to have it.

Within a few weeks, I started getting regular welfare checks. It was not much, just $250 per month, so I had to be careful with my budgeting. After paying my $150 monthly rent, I used the rest for transportation and other things I could not buy with my $100 monthly allotment of food stamps. Welfare assistance also helped me pay for English immersion classes at NOVA through a program offering refugees education grants and job training. The government subsidies covered my child-care costs while I was in school all day, and the welfare office even helped register my new babysitter—a Filipino woman named Trish who lived in my new apartment building—so she could get paid directly by the appropriate government agency.

In some ways, moving to the suburbs had improved my situation. I had a safe, clean apartment; I was close to a reliable friend; and I had a steady income. Even with those things working in my favor, my situation was less than ideal. I still needed the hand-me-down clothes. And in the back of my mind, I could not keep from thinking, You have gone from three jobs to no jobs, to failing out of trade school, and now you're living on welfare.

It was not my lowest point, but I still felt stuck and unable to make any progress towards a stable career. The only thing that had changed for me over the past nine months was the scenery. I was growing impatient, and my self-esteem was becoming more fragile. My vulnerability made me the perfect target for men to take advantage of me. The struggle to protect my children and myself became even harder.

After moving to Virginia, given the delicate state of my mind and emotions, I was not looking for love; I was only interested in survival. My track record with men in America seemed to suggest I was destined to be treated like either a princess or a prostitute, and I had no way of knowing which of those roles any given man intended for me to play. Still, I must have been giving off "save me" signals, because it seemed like the number of men with whom I came into contact increased exponentially—especially since I was attending classes at a large community college. Although Chuong was on his guard, he was far from pressuring me into a relationship, so other men approached me at will.

Like at La Cave, I met a broad group of diverse people at NOVA. Everyone was very friendly and quick to help me acclimate to the campus. My classmates gathered once or twice a week for social events. And my professor was especially nice to me. Whenever I stayed after class to ask questions, which was most days, he patiently answered every one. He knew a great deal about the plight of refugees, and knowing I was a single mom who had just entered the welfare system, he went out of his way to help me, even more than the other students.

I had been at NOVA for a few months when Chuong showed the first signs of jealousy. He began to express concern that men in my class were being a little too nice to me. When he found out that my professor had asked me out to dinner, Chuong insisted he had some perverse motive for giving me such special attention. He was probably right. But I didn't understand why this bothered Chuong, since he was away most of the week.

My professor and classmates should have been the least of Chuong's worries. I was meeting other men in other places and through other people, unrelated to school. These men might have threatened his hero status more than my English teacher. That is, if I had been focused on romance at all.

One gentleman was a lawyer who worked on Capitol Hill, writing briefs for a congressman. He had been a regular customer at Arabian Nights. He lived in D.C., and once took a taxi into Virginia to pick me up. From there we headed back into the city to the Kennedy Center to see the symphony. But for some reason, I was fixated on why he was not a judge yet. In my ignorance of the profession, I figured if he went to law school, he should aspire to become a judge instead of working on Capitol Hill.

At the end of one date, I asked him, "Why aren't you a judge?" He must have taken it to heart, or he just really wanted to impress me, because he left Capitol Hill and moved out west. Several months later, he called to tell me he had become a judge in Arizona as the result of our conversation. It took me years to understand the impact we had on each other.

Another man in my life was a businessman and multi-millionaire from Pennsylvania. Jerry was a distinguished man in his late fifties. In many ways, he reminded me of Fox. In addition to being successful in business, Jerry was an inventor and philanthropist who regularly ate lunch at a restaurant in Washington, D.C. where my half-sister Chi worked. Like most wealthy philanthropists, Jerry was interested in finding another worthy cause to which he might direct his resources and attention. He had just read about the large number of Vietnamese refugees in the area and asked Chi if she knew anyone who needed help. Chi told Jerry about her refugee sister, who had two children and was struggling to get established in Virginia. Instantly intrigued, he asked for my phone number.

"I understand you're a refugee and need help," said a kindly voice when I answered the phone. "My name is Jerry. Your sister may have told you I'd be calling. I hoped we might be able to meet. I'd like to know how I can be of assistance."

"Thank you," I said. "If you want to help me, take me to the grocery store."

Finding a reliable babysitter remained one of my biggest challenges. It's a dilemma to which all single working parents can relate. If I wanted to go anywhere, even on a quick trip to the store, I had to take both kids. And with no car, I would have to carry the groceries and two kids back home, making this seemingly basic errand prohibitively complicated. Given my situation, the biggest favor someone could do for me was give me a ride.

"I think I can do that," he said.

On that first trip to the grocery store, Jerry offered to pay, but I politely declined, proudly retrieving the food stamps from my purse. I wanted to show him I would not take advantage of his kindness.

The grocery store trip was the first of countless favors Jerry would do for my children and me. He frequently came to town from his estate outside of Philadelphia to take me out to lunch or dinner— sometimes with the kids, sometimes just the two of us. Occasionally, he would send small amounts of money for me to buy the kids clothes or myself a dress. He was never pushy, just friendly and caring.

If Chuong was like a protective older brother, Jerry was a doting father. Soon he started taking the kids and me on his business trips to New York. We toured the city, window-shopped at all the big department stores, and lunched atop the World Trade Center. I was as much in awe of the city as Bang and Mai were. At night Jerry would hire a sitter to watch the kids at our hotel while he took me out to explore the city's best attractions. He introduced me to people and places I could only have dreamed about without him. He once even offered to take us on a trip around the world, but I had to decline because I was still in school. For those amazing experiences and his generosity, I am truly thankful to him.

Jerry's kindness never came with even the slightest hint of expectations or romantic notions. Then one day, about halfway through a dinner together, he got down on one knee and asked me to marry him.

It was a shock.

Marrying for love has always been the most important thing to me. For me, a person can be the richest in the world, but to be with someone without loving them would be miserable. I believe love is the only thing that can bring true happiness.

"Jerry, I love you ... but not in that way," I said, trying to find the right expression and hide my complete astonishment. "I don't think I should marry you. I don't think I'm the right person. I don't love you the way you want me to love you. You deserve a lot more than I'm able to give you." He kissed my hand and said, "You're a very nice girl. When you finally do marry, you don't want to struggle, so don't marry poor."

I thought, *You're not the first person to tell me that.*

While Chuong continued to play the role of an over-protective older brother, I continued to casually date. The most serious threat to Chuong's long-term agenda was an American named Rob—a Dartmouth graduate who worked for the Peace Corps, where he learned to speak fluent Vietnamese. He was very kind to my children and me. And unlike Chuong, he was completely upfront about his feelings for me and where he wanted our relationship to go.

What attracted me most to Rob was how he understood me. He saw the strength and desire in me to provide a better life for my children. "I see you as Scarlett O'Hara," he once told me. "You're strong, tough, and beautiful. Your attitude is always to say, 'Tomorrow is another day.'" I had never seen or read *Gone with the Wind*, and the words probably lost something in translation, but when he repeated the sentiments in Vietnamese, it made me smile.

I think Rob also wanted to protect me. Understanding the Vietnamese culture, he knew better than to be too forward with me too soon. But his actions made it very clear that he would help take care of my kids and me. He truly loved me and eventually said as much. While I knew and felt all of this, I didn't have the same romantic feelings for him. He was determined and reassured me that, while he understood my feelings, he could make me love him if I would only agree to marry him.

I introduced Rob to everyone I knew, and they all loved him—everyone but Chuong, of course. In retrospect, I understand why, but at the time, I only knew Chuong did not want me to marry a Caucasian.

"The only Asian who would marry a white guy is a prostitute," he said. "You need to marry a good Vietnamese man."

I had heard the "white devil" propaganda most of my life in Vietnam, and since leaving my homeland, I had done my best to avoid the abysmal life of a prostitute. So Chuong's words cut deep. But I didn't accept them outright. Instead, I told Rob what Chuong said and asked what he thought about the long-term prospects for a relationship between a single, never-married white man and a single Vietnamese mother.

To his credit, Rob stood firm. "With you," he said, "I've met the girl of my dreams." I was skeptical and asked him many questions based on what Chuong said. Rob was extremely caring and open about his intentions.

He proposed. I declined.

Mr. Brick and Jerry were probably somewhere shaking their heads at yet another missed opportunity for me to marry well. Would it have made my life and my kids' lives easier to marry Rob? Probably. At least for a while. But I have no regrets. I never expected my life to be easy. I just wanted it to be my own life, on my terms. I wanted it all: true love, a great job, and the freedom to be myself. My life with Rob might have been easier, since he was very well off, but I knew it was not right to marry someone I didn't love.

At the end of the fall semester in 1976, Chuong persuaded me to leave NOVA and return to trade school. He said I was ready. Having a full English class under my belt and wanting to get back on the career track as soon as possible, I didn't need much convincing. I also did not take Chuong's pressuring me to leave NOVA as anything more than continued encouragement to reach my goal of becoming a secretary. I was not yet tuned into his insecurities or controlling ways.

In the fall, I enrolled in ITT Tech, ready (if not so eager) to give shorthand another go. While in school, I didn't work. Welfare continued to cover my rent, tuition, and childcare during school hours. Mr. Brick (and sometimes Jerry) helped to fill in the gaps.

Whenever I visited Mr. Brick, he would treat me to lunch or dinner. Unsolicited, he sometimes gave me $100 or more, saying the money was for treating Bang and Mai to ice cream. Whatever I had left over from Mr. Brick's exorbitant ice cream fund went towards other, more essential items—such as milk, bread, and clothing (okay, and makeup).

After a bumpy first year in the U.S., I went back to secretarial school. My English had improved a little in my short time at NOVA, and I was ready to get back on track to becoming an independent woman with a sustainable career. Though my teachers were supportive, one of my half-sisters was not. I invited her to my apartment for lunch one day, assuming she would be proud to hear that I was working towards something substantial. Instead, she responded with contempt.

"You didn't speak English when you arrived, and you can barely speak it now," she said. "You've got two kids to feed and no skills, and now you're in some school for secretaries? What are you doing here?"

I had no worthy defense. If her first brutal comments bruised my spirit, the next drew blood. "How are you ever going to earn a living here? Unless you're willing to sleep for money. Or maybe you can find someone willing to marry you—but who would want you with your two children?"

While I may not have known exactly what I wanted to do just yet, I absolutely knew what I didn't want to do. This made her comment sting even more. She was saying I should give up and throw away my aspirations and dignity for some easy money. The little confidence I had managed to develop during the previous few months at school now lay in shreds on my dining room floor. I wondered, *What if she's right?*

Desperate people often make desperate choices. For that reason, they often make the wrong ones. The boys and girls I had become familiar with down on 14th Street may have been forced into making their desperate choices by circumstances beyond their control. As they spiraled downward, maybe there was nothing left for them to lose but hope, and that's when the temptation to take the "easy" way out may have been most powerful. Drugs, alcohol, prostitution or even suicide might have seemed like the only options available to them—the only possible escape from their already tragic narratives. As a struggling single parent with no job and no money, I began to understand how a cycle of negative thinking could destroy a person's spirit—or even the will to live.

When I had first enrolled at La Cave, I had all the energy and optimism in the world. Now at ITT, I doubted my ability to succeed. My psyche was ready to crumble. My thoughts veered towards self-destruction. I wish I could say this was the only time it would happen to me, but I would be lying. This first time, someone unexpected intervened at just the right moment.

The week after my half-sister's visit, I sat in class sobbing while I was supposed to be learning a new language (shorthand) in another language I still barely understood. At the end of one class, my teacher asked me what was wrong.

"I just want to die," I said.

Her response probably saved my life. "You don't want to die," she said. "You can't. If you do, who's going to suffer? Your kids, that's who. And your parents. It doesn't matter what anyone else tells you. Just keep going. You're going to make it because you have to!"

She was right. Giving up on myself meant giving up on my kids. I had to shift my attention from my own feelings of despair, back to my responsibility for their survival and their future. Also in the back of my mind were my parents and family in Vietnam. I had to succeed if I was ever going to bring them over and give them a new start. And if I quit on them all, who else would be there for them?

Instead of dwelling on my difficult situation or blaming myself for it, I had to use this bout of adversity as a catalyst to create something good and meaningful for my family. For my children and their survival, I was willing to sacrifice anything.

I finished classes at ITT after nine months but didn't graduate, because I failed my shorthand course again. On the other hand, I had gained a better attitude and outlook, fueled by my teacher's timely words, which I have never forgotten.

Soon after I finished at ITT, Mr. Brick called and asked me to come to his office. He wanted to hire me as an executive assistant. When I started a couple of weeks later, everyone at his office was extremely nice and supportive of me. But I had not even made it to lunchtime before my nemesis—shorthand—reared its ugly head and exposed my fatal weakness. If I could not take dictation, it just was not going to work out for me as Mr. Brick's or anyone else's secretary.

I felt stupid. And I found myself in yet another quandary: I needed to improve my English in order to succeed in business, but Chuong was not going to let me return to NOVA for the classes I needed. Instead, he encouraged me to go to beauty school, like his sister had. I had met her once before and found her impressive. She dressed nicely and had a good job at Elizabeth Arden, so I agreed to give beauty school a try.

Though it was good advice, which I would not regret taking, Chuong's suggestion did not come from a purely helpful place. He thought that if I became a secretary, I would be surrounded by men. "If you worked in an office, you'd be sexually harassed," he insisted. After he had diverted my career aspirations and torpedoed my relationships with Rob and other men, Chuong quit his job in New Jersey, came back to Virginia, applied for welfare like I had, and tried to go back to school himself. It was then that his dominance over me started to grow less subtle and caring, but still, I listened to him. He had my undivided attention.

We were both single parents. He had been married twice before and had three daughters—one with his first wife and two with the second. One daughter, Jackie, was left behind in Vietnam with his second wife; the other two, Ann and Karen, lived with him in the U.S. He already treated Bang and Mai as if they were his own and had grown very protective of them. Because we shared the same cultural background and economic circumstances, I believed that Chuong and I understood and could help each other. He was good to us, but it would become clear to me years later that I was also becoming the one thing in his life he could control.

I opted for the security of shared culture and his promise to take care of me. I didn't realize that, despite my desire to be independent and self-sufficient, I was actually letting Chuong make my decisions for me. At the time, I saw only a kind-hearted, caring man who had my best interests in mind.

Everything during my first two years in America seemed designed to knock me down. But like that bumblebee defying the odds, I proceeded to beat my wings even faster. It was my nature. Despite the repeated setbacks, I kept finding a way to stay airborne. This time it would be Monique Beauty Academy.

Chapter 9: *Lather, Rinse, Repeat*

Chuong's idea for me to attend beauty school made perfect sense to me. The idea of helping women feel pretty—feel better about themselves—rekindled in me an ember of desire, one which had all but been extinguished in the years since I had posed among the *vu sua* trees of Kon Tum and exchanged beauty secrets with Fox's girlfriend.

My life was a mess. I had failed in the U.S. by most academic, economic, and social measures. I was single, a secretarial-school dropout, and living on welfare. But I always made sure I looked "together." I carefully styled my hair and applied makeup every morning, even for trips to the grocery store. I dressed well and kept my mostly donated clothes clean and pressed. No matter how I felt and no matter what the day might bring, I always seemed to possess the power to transform self-doubt into self-confidence with the stroke of an eye pencil and turn of a comb. My attention to my appearance was not just about aesthetics; it was about overcoming feelings of inadequacy. Looking good made me feel good about myself.

Knowing how to apply makeup and style hair has served me well personally as well as professionally. These skills have helped me retain a sense of control over how the world perceives me and how I feel about myself. And at times, I have felt invincible because of them.

The thought of providing similar moments of self-satisfaction and power to other women was an attractive, even inspirational, prospect. Could entering beauty school finally be the positive turning point I had been looking for?

Regardless of his motives, with his suggestion, Chuong had reinvigorated a part of me that, until then, was only a faint glimmer beneath the eyeliner and second-hand clothing I took pride in wearing each day. What was once a whisper of interest was now loudly encouraging me to help other women not only to look good, but also feel as if they could go anywhere, accomplish anything, and turn heads in the process.

I entered Monique Beauty Academy energized by the thought that, within a year, I could become a fully-licensed cosmetologist. My confidence grew even more when I discovered I already knew many of the things we would be studying. And the icing on the cake was that my English aptitude had little bearing on whether I excelled in beauty school. I learned just fine by watching the instructors, asking questions, and imitating what they did. Because I was working more with my hands and was not as intimidated by the coursework, the new skills came more easily to me than anything I had attempted at La Cave.

The learning environment at Monique was also more pleasant for me. The instructors, as well as the students, were from diverse, international backgrounds. I felt comfortable for a change, and I let myself get excited about being a student again.

After two trade-school failures, emerging from Monique with a degree in 1978 gave me my first sense of achievement since coming to the U.S. It was surprisingly easy to begin putting my degree to use. But my up-and-down days weren't over yet. I would soon learn the beauty business can be volatile.

In the late fall of 1979, I accepted a $150-per-week position at Salon Jean Paul, which was located inside Garfinkel's, a department store at Springfield Mall in Northern Virginia. Chuong taught me how to drive and sold me a used Renault for $700 so that I could get to work on my own. It felt good to be regaining some independence, and my confidence continued plodding its way upward towards daylight.

At the bottom of the salon pecking order is the shampoo girl. I was a stylist's assistant, which was just one step up. On the plus side, my boss

Regis was extremely successful, not only in a business sense, but also as a stylist. He often took in more than $1,000 a day from his chair alone. Working under him would be a great learning experience.

From the minute I entered his salon, I closely studied the way Regis handled himself as a manager, as well as how he wielded the tools of his trade with the artistry and precision of an illusionist. Like a magician, his performances were always met by the appreciative "oohs" and "ahhs" of a multitude of loyal customers, mostly women. I wanted to be like him—not just a business success, but to also have my talents admired and appreciated by customers and colleagues.

Regis hired me to replace one of his assistants who had taken a leave of absence to train for the summer Olympics. She was a swimmer and, like his other two assistants, she was blond-haired, blue-eyed, and statuesque. When I began working there, I was the only flat-nosed, slant-eyed person on the staff. To compensate for my differences, I tried to dress nicely and treat everyone as politely as possible.

Despite my efforts to be part of the team, I stood out—and not necessarily in the way I would have liked. The other girls, even those beneath me in the salon pecking order, frequently teased me with an overly pronounced Asian accent, alternating between calls of "ah-so" and "asshole." I didn't understand. They had branded me as Chinese (as if that would have made their racist teasing more acceptable). Like the majority of Americans in the seventies, they could not—or would not— distinguish between different Asian cultures. So when mocking us, the same stereotypical accent applied to all.

While I knew the teasing and behind-my-back snickering was mean spirited, I never stopped long enough to consider whether their malice was derived from misplaced jealousy, blind resentment or just fear of the unknown. It didn't matter, and I didn't have the time to waste getting distracted by close-minded people and their childish games.

I was there to earn, learn, and then move on when a better opportunity came along. And the thirty-percent discount on Garfinkle's merchandise was nice too.

⁂

In contrast to the pettiness routinely displayed by my co-workers, my customers often provided me with a glimpse of the best people had to offer. One regular client, whom I had gotten to know over many hours of washing and drying, showed up early to her appointment one day around Christmas.

After our many chat sessions, she knew most of my story and that I had kids. She also knew I didn't make much money as a hairdresser's assistant and probably was not able to afford a seventy-five-dollar gift like the one she carried into the salon in a giant, colorfully wrapped box. It was a Star Trek Enterprise toy for Bang.

In Vietnam there are no thank you notes. If someone gives you a gift, you express your gratitude in the moment and then spend weeks thinking about how to repay them later. The toy was yet another beautiful act of kindness, performed for me by yet another beautiful stranger I was never able to adequately repay.

When almost everything about my work environment told me I didn't belong, it always seemed to be a customer's kind gesture that encouraged me and let me know I was right where I was supposed to be at the time.

⁂

The blond swimmer returned after just a few months. The U.S. was boycotting the 1980 Olympic Games. With no plans to compete, training was cut short, and American athletes were sent home early. Shortly thereafter, Regis let me go. I cried, taking it as another personal failure. Apparently the tall, blond swimmer and I shared something in common after all—the major disappointment of being prematurely dismissed. In a way, a symbolic stand against communism cost me my first real job—just as it had cost me my home in Vietnam.

My kind mentor, however, didn't just send me on my way empty-handed. Instead, Regis provided personal introductions and recommendations at a few other local salons—including at a Lord & Taylor located just a few miles from my apartment.

Also an upscale salon, Lord & Taylor hired me as an entry-level hairdresser, giving me my first chance to actually cut hair. As a stylist's assistant, I had always dressed the part of an actual stylist—perfect coif, perfect nails, and perfect makeup. I was eager for my dress rehearsal to be over and to finally begin building relationships with my own customers.

The first clue my experience at Lord & Taylor might not be all I hoped for was the clientele—which was much older than at Regis's salon. I was used to dressing and styling myself to look more like my customers, which was hard to do when surrounded by people more than twice my age. My next clue was that, other than the few friends who knew about my new job, the number of customers flowing my way was barely a trickle. Five days a week, from 9:00 a.m. to 6:00 p.m., I tried to learn more and get established, but something seemed "off," and I didn't think it was just because I was the new girl.

With a little investigating, I soon uncovered the truth about why my chair was gathering dust instead of derrieres. By more closely observing the interactions between customers and the salon's receptionist—the person responsible for directing walk-ins to available hairdressers—I noticed mine was always the last chair filled, if it was filled at all. Although it made sense for senior hairdressers to receive precedence over newcomers like me, my chair often remained empty while new customers waited, regardless of whether they had requested another stylist. When this receptionist was working, I had to repeatedly ask to have business sent my way; otherwise I was ignored. I would later discover the receptionist was also skimming money from my tips.

Unfortunately, the opportunity at Lord & Taylor was short-lived. After three months, I was "offered" a transfer to another, busier store in Chevy Chase, Maryland. But the location was more than fifteen miles from my home, which was too far for someone who had barely begun to drive. To make such a commute every day in city traffic would have made my already hectic schedule unbearable. I reluctantly declined the transfer, even though it meant being on the job hunt again. But this time it was easier to look on the bright side. Now that I had my hairdresser's license and some good experience, I knew I could weather this and any future "failure" without having to start all over again. In fact, I could actually advance.

The search for a new chair only took as long as a quick visit with Regis, whose list of contacts and job leads was endless. He suggested I meet with a woman named Mylandre, who owned a large stand-alone salon just up the street from Lord & Taylor. She currently had only one hairdresser on staff and was looking to hire someone. Again Regis's recommendation was all I needed to impress her, and I began work that week. New customers came quickly and I knew right away I would be much happier there.

After about three months, Mylandre hired an assistant— another tall blonde—to work with me. Putting in long hours together, it didn't take long for me and the new assistant to become friends. Over the next nine months, she got to know me, my kids, and our story very well. I even invited her to family gatherings, including my birthday party. I still have pictures of us enjoying those events, smiling with our arms around each other like the best of friends.

I felt I had gained another ally in my fight to establish myself as a stylist and earn respect in the business. I was wrong.

One busy evening around 7:30 p.m., as I finished with a customer, I was already running late to pick up my kids from the babysitter. I didn't have time to clean my station but knew I could do so the next morning before the salon opened. I grabbed my purse and hurried home.

The next morning, I got to work at my usual time and began cleaning and preparing my station for the day. I casually reached to open my drawer and retrieve some supplies. The drawer would usually glide open with minimal effort, but that morning I needed two hands to coax it, inch by inch, out of its slot. Thousands of thick, downy tufts of brown, charcoal, and golden hair bulged over the drawer's edge and fell at my feet in dusty clumps. Apparently the assistant decided to clean up the hair around my station for me. I had been blindsided by the shampoo girl!

As upset as I was, I knew I needed to calm down before talking to the owner. It took me twenty minutes to clean up the mess, but instead of the cooling-down effect I had hoped for, the wasted time only intensified my anger. As shocked as I had been by my friend's betrayal, I was equally surprised when Mylandre simply brushed off the situation. Instead of standing up for one of her top-dollar stylists in the face of serious insubordination by a new assistant, Mylandre said, "Don't worry about it," and did nothing.

I was speechless. Not because I could not formulate the words in English. I could not find the words in any language. I let my feet do the talking and walked out, never to return.

I did not feel that I could impose on Regis again so soon. I needed to find my next job by myself. One afternoon I set out to survey Northern Virginia's salon landscape—or at least the landscape along Route 7, which stretched westward to Tyson's Corner.

I had only been driving for the short twelve months since moving to the Virginia suburbs. While I did not want my job search to be aimless, I also didn't want to get lost. Thirty minutes into my drive, while passing through downtown Falls Church, a sign caught my eye: Beau Monde (French for "Beautiful World"). It was an oasis wedged into the middle of an ordinary strip mall—one I had probably passed hundreds of times without a second glance. But on that morning, the floor-to-ceiling windows draped in sheer silk caught the light just right and seemed to beckon me in from the street. I doubt I would ever have noticed the salon otherwise, but now that I did, I somehow knew I had found the right place for me. I hoped the owner knew it too.

I strode through the parking lot towards Beau Monde, hardly able to contain my smile. The towering windows had stylish drapes instead of the usual venetian blinds. The openness allowed me to see, even from the parking lot, several customers seated along one wall of the all-white interior. *The place looks busy, elegant, and clean,* I thought. *This is good.* Upon entering, I could see why so many customers were waiting. There was only one hairdresser working. This was also good. Beau Monde met the most important of all my criteria: needs stylist.

While the waiting women mindlessly thumbed through months-old fashion magazines, occasionally glancing at a clock over the door, the lone stylist carried on a cheery conversation with the woman beneath her shears. After a minute, she noticed me standing in the doorway. She politely asked me to come in and then nodded to the last empty chair, inviting me to sit down. Still smiling, I asked, "May I see the manager, please?"

With her eyes never leaving her syncopated scissors and comb, which rapidly sheared and ejected curls and split ends to the floor, the stylist called over her shoulder, "Raheleh!" After a pause, she returned my smile and said, "If you'd like to have a seat, she'll be right with you." Her eyes, comb, and shears returned to the precision pruning.

Raheleh had a style all her own. I suppose the same could be said of any accomplished artist or anyone who's found long-term success in the salon business. But as an Iranian woman taking advantage of her American freedom and contradicting her native culture's oppressive norms, Raheleh stood out. She was flawless, with the chiseled bone structure and tiny waist of a model. Her eyes were green, lips tiny, skin perfect, bosom ample and energy level high.

Punctuating her already striking appearance was a bountiful head of bleached-blond hair, which somehow reflected a purple tint (a look she achieved by treating her hair virtually one strand at a time). You didn't just notice when Raheleh entered a room; you felt it. With her startling looks and velvety accent, she reminded me of Zsa Zsa Gabor in her prime. She was also warm, friendly and not at all intimidating. I liked her immediately.

The feeling, apparently, was mutual. Raheleh instantly hired me as her second stylist. In most salons, stylists "eat what they kill" and pay a percentage to the owners, not including tips. So I would basically be a small-business owner, renting the real estate taken up by my station— a business within a business, so to speak. After some negotiations, Raheleh and I agreed I would keep sixty percent of the money I brought in, which was generous, as the normal split for beginning stylists was fifty-fifty.

"When can I begin?" I asked, trying my best not to sound overeager.

"Whenever you like," she said.

I told her I would be back in two days.

Ever since my early days in the salon business, I've had three lessons about success reinforced for me. First, everyone you meet is a potential resource. Second, every resource is valuable. Third, people do business with people they like.

These lessons are particularly true for anyone entering a new profession. Throughout my decades in business, I have shared this with everyone I mentored: No matter how modest your network of family, friends, neighbors, and acquaintances, you should never be shy about tapping into it. While this may seem obvious to many in today's social-networking society, as a novice in the business world, this was a revelation to me.

As I began building my client base in the late seventies and early eighties, I reminded myself that there is no shame in reaching out to friends. Within just a few days of starting at Beau Monde, I had contacted nearly everyone I knew in the D.C. area. I talked to not only my close friends and past clients, but also to people with whom I had just recently made connections. I kept every business card, napkin, and scrap of paper with a phone number on it, thinking every new person I met could one day become a client or a referral source. It was a primitive version of Facebook or LinkedIn—more time-consuming, but just as effective. Some might say even more effective, as the personal bonds I created and strengthened back then have endured for decades.

My first call after accepting the new job was to my dear friend Tuan Nguyen. In addition to being one of the first friends I made in Virginia, Tuan had the distinction of being my original "client" while I was still in beauty school.

Always complimentary of my work, Tuan was fond of telling people, "When Rosemary does your hair, you don't just come out looking different. You are a different person. She's that good."

I met Tuan when I joined the Holy Martyrs of Vietnam Catholic Church in Arlington, Virginia. A devout Christian who has dedicated her life to lifting up others in need, Tuan got to know me and my story almost from the instant I walked into the church. She had worked with Voice of America in Vietnam during the war and was able to move with her job to the U.S. afterwards. She stayed on with the network for a few more years until she opened a successful dry-cleaning business in Northern Virginia, followed by four electronics stores. She later returned to government work, becoming a teacher with the Virginia Department of Social Services Office of Newcomer Services, where she helped support the resettlement of refugees from Vietnam, Latin America, and other areas ravaged by war.

Having remained single all her life, Tuan watched over my kids and me as if we were her own. She quickly became the most positive influence in my life—a mentor, spiritual guide, and more. She helped connect me to others in the church congregation, many of whom became clients. Her older brother Cuong taught Bang how to play violin well enough to eventually earn a seat in his college symphony orchestra. She even co-signed the lease for my first apartment in Virginia. More importantly, Tuan became godmother to Mai and a second mother to me, as well as another angel in my life. I am always counting my blessings for knowing her.

My next call was to another woman who would have a profound impact on the rest of my American life. Arlene Heinzman had been my client at Mylandre and quickly became a friend. Twenty years after I first cut her hair, she would write the business plan for my nonprofit organization, Devotion to Children. I believe God brought me to the beauty industry and the industry in turn brought Arlene and many more special individuals to me—and, by extension, to the organization that would become my life's work.

As I got to know Raheleh, I realized we were destined to meet. While in Iran and after coming to the U.S., Raheleh had suffered through numerous failed marriages. In fact, her list of ex-husbands rivals Elizabeth Taylor's. On the one hand, she had enjoyed a life of privilege in her country, because her family was extremely wealthy. But as a woman in her culture, she had also endured more than her share of oppression.

During my rewarding time working at Beau Monde, I learned how to be a great stylist and also a true entrepreneur. I even took a second job working a few hours three nights a week at Adrianne Arpel in Bloomingdale's, where I administered facial treatments and sold cosmetics. I wanted to become a more well-rounded beauty professional (Raheleh was the skincare expert at Beau Monde and exclusively handled all facials) and gain greater exposure to the store's upscale clientele. I was again working two jobs, but this time it was something I truly enjoyed—something with a real future.

One of my regulars at Beau Monde and her husband were a fairly well-to-do couple who owned a restaurant in Georgetown. One day the woman told me they'd just sold the restaurant and asked if I would be interested in partnering with her to open a new salon. With my advanced skills and growing ambition, it was only natural that I would eventually leave Beau Monde to start my own business. I just had not expected the opportunity to come around so soon. I had no money to invest.

When I explained this, she said, "Well, I have the money, and you have the expertise. Why don't I buy one, and we can be partners?" She was asking if I wanted to own my own business, be my own boss, and make good money doing what I love. Of course I did.

❧

As exciting as it was to start my first business, an even bigger life change was on the horizon. After moving to Virginia, I had grown even closer to Chuong. He quit his job in New Jersey to spend more time with the kids and me. Before he quit, our families were only together on the weekends when I was not working. I began to miss him as much as he said he missed me.

Chuong was thirteen years older than me, extremely reliable, and very protective. He made us all feel safe when he was around, and I always felt he gave me the respect I deserved. But even as we were becoming like members of a single family who just happened to live in separate apartments, I still viewed Chuong as more of a friend than a love interest. We took care of each other. This was all I thought I needed. I remained focused on advancing my career and providing for my kids.

My relationship with Chuong might have stayed in the same, comfortable place—just friends—had it not been for his mother. Having Chuong out of town most of the week when I first moved to Virginia allowed me to grow close to his parents, especially his mother. She was a proud woman with quiet strength. Her name in Vietnamese literally meant "moon," which suited her perfectly. Though never a pushover, she was gentle and loving, and I admired her very much.

By the time Chuong's mother arrived in the U.S., she was already in her seventies and, like many refugees, was penniless. Even at her advanced age, she insisted on earning her keep, despite having her son and welfare to provide any necessities. To make her own money, she cooked traditional Vietnamese dishes and carried them, as if she were a caterer, to various fairs, farmers' markets, and other local events where she could make a modest profit.

Soft spoken as she was, Chuong's mother also was known for being direct. The older one gets, the easier this is to do, I suppose. One day while we were alone, she told me, "You have no husband and two kids. He has no wife and two kids. Don't you think it just makes sense for you to marry him?" It was probably the most rational proposal I had ever gotten.

When I stopped to consider our situation as objectively as she had, I knew she was right. In addition to my close relationship with Chuong, I had grown to love his girls, who were always very sweet. Bang and Mai loved them too. I also believed what Chuong had been telling me for years: "No one will take care of your children like I will." Despite working part time and not earning as much as I was, Chuong stayed true to his word, spending his spare time helping to care for my children. These things made my decision easy.

In the spring of 1982, a year after his mother intervened and after clearing up a few unresolved issues to finally close the book on both our previous marriages, Chuong and I exchanged vows. I now had two older daughters, which meant Bang and Mai had two older sisters who could play with and help take care of them.

Going against Mr. Brick's advice (and much to the delight of my new mother-in-law), I decided to marry for love rather than money.

La Madeleine, my other new partnership, opened for business just a few months after the wedding. The salon was situated in the busy shopping area of Bailey's Crossroads, a great location for customer traffic. The salon's French name reflected the European style and sophisticated elegance my new partner and I wanted to deliver to our customers. Like other upscale salons with French flair that had been growing in popularity, such as Alexandre de Paris and Claude de Paris, we aspired to pamper clients with more than just basic hairstyling, manicure and pedicure services. We planned to someday offer a full-service spa experience. And for a while, things looked very promising as we slowly worked towards this goal.

I brought most of my clients over from Beau Monde and Adrienne Arpel. La Madeleine turned a profit within the first three months of operation. In a short time, we had already surpassed the average monthly profits of the previous owner, who had been in business for more than twenty-five years.

For the first eight months, the business seemed to be moving along smoothly from my perspective. I began looking for ways to further increase our sales, including selling more high-end, high-profit-margin hair and skin products. When I told my partner that I would need money to buy these from a wholesaler, she cautioned me that La Madeleine was low on cash. I did not understand how cash flow could be a problem; I was busier than ever with customers, and we almost always had a waiting list. To give us a quick cash infusion and further increase our customer traffic, I suggested bringing in another partner. My partner agreed.

Our third partner was someone I knew from working at Bloomingdale's. She had sharp skills, good experience, and understood the demands of upscale clients. Just as importantly, she had money to invest. I was confident she would complement the style and vision we had established for La Madeleine.

Then one day in the spring of 1983, I found out the truth about La Madeleine's money crunch. Earlier that day, I had given a customer a dye job. She paid in cash but when I later went to count out the cash drawer, I discovered the money and receipt were gone. For the next week or two, I paid closer attention to the money I was taking in to see if this was just a one-time mistake or if something else was going on.

I discovered the "something else" was partner number one. At this time I was eight months pregnant and certainly didn't need the added stress. I knew I would have to confront her right away—for the sake of the business and my own peace of mind. The next day, when I asked my partner about the missing cash, she reluctantly admitted "borrowing" money from the salon's profits to help keep up with the cost of her son's private schooling. Apparently, she had been borrowing money almost since the salon opened.

I told her I had trusted her with the books and that she had betrayed my trust. She did not apologize and did not seem to feel she had done anything wrong. Things went downhill from there. I felt my expertise was responsible for building our impressive client list. Taking cash from the business without telling me was not good business practice. My partner could not see that this caused me to lose respect for her. I'd had enough of being ripped off, being kept in the dark, and having my hard-earned money stolen from under my nose.

With everything out in the open, the three of us agreed a change was necessary. To my surprise, my partners' solution was more drastic than anything I would ever have considered. We all figured the salon's assets were about $30,000. Each of us had put up $3,000 for a partnership share. The two of them offered to buy me out—for $1,500. Instead of apologizing or agreeing to stop embezzling money from the business for which I brought in most of the money, they made it clear I should go.

My only response was to say it was more logical for me to retain ownership. I didn't have much money, but given their math, surely I could afford the $3,000 to buy them out. A day later, with both competing offers still on the table, I arrived at the salon to find my partners had changed the locks. They would not even let me in to collect my belongings, including some styling tools, a few pictures, some clothing and fabric, and my wedding band, which I had removed earlier in the day while giving a client a facial. They put my belongings into a trash bag and dropped it on my doorstep.

I was no lawyer, but I knew this was not right. I was the heart and soul of La Madeleine, and I was certain the salon would not survive without me—which turned out to be true. Within a year of my leaving, my former partners sold the salon. I was finally reimbursed and bought a pair of nice earrings with the money.

This was not the first time I had left someplace under extreme circumstances, but it stung nonetheless. I had been kicked out as if I were the one who had done something wrong. I had seen something happening that was not right, spoke up, and was severely punished for doing so. Making matters worse, I could not just move on to a new job. Who was going to hire a pregnant woman in her third trimester? As bad as the timing was and as big a setback as it seemed, I could not afford to panic or dwell on any of it. Chuong and I were about to have our first child together. Anh was on her way, and I was not going to allow anything to complicate her arrival. Because Chuong was only working part time, I could not quit working entirely. All I needed was another silver lining ... and a chair.

୶

It was springtime—a time for new beginnings. I accepted my circumstances and set my mind to adapting to them as quickly as I could. Given my profession, this was relatively easy to do. I began styling hair from my basement. I set up a makeshift salon workstation beside my laundry room sink—using a dining room chair, an old dresser with propped-up mirror, a beat-up, reclining shampooing chair (which I had reclaimed from the trash heap behind a barber shop), and a five-gallon bucket to catch the water. It was not Beau Monde and it didn't have elegant draperies, but it worked.

When my clients discovered I had left La Madeleine, most of them came looking for me. I lost a few during the transition, but because the clients I kept (God bless them all) offered to keep paying my salon rates, and I was not splitting my earnings with two partners, my income did not change much. Though I realized I could not work from home forever and still grow my business, I was satisfied with the temporary arrangement. It allowed me to work a full-time schedule after Anh was born.

Anh was so small and precious. I had difficulty giving birth to her, however, because her head was too large. The doctors had to use suction in order to pull her out, which burst a few blood vessels in her head, causing it to swell to a disproportionately large size. The nine days she had to stay in the hospital were perhaps the longest of my life. I cried every day when I got to see her and was so happy when I could finally bring her home.

Working from home, I was blessed to see all my children every day after school. And my new stepdaughters were such a blessing. Ann, the oldest, helped me shampoo clients' hair and also made dinner for the family. Meanwhile, Karen helped take care of her three younger siblings.

Being kicked out by my partners—people I had trusted and considered friends—broke my heart. It had come at the worst possible time for my family. It was traumatic, cruel, and unfair. But with a little faith and luck, and a lot of determination, something positive was about to come out of a horribly unfortunate situation.

The day my La Madeleine partners dumped my belongings on my doorstep as if they were nothing but trash to be thrown out, I was reminded of the old saying, "The best revenge is living well." I had become an old pro at dealing with tough situations, which made it easier to reassure myself I would be a stronger person for it and that all this was happening for a good reason. It would not take long for me to discover that reason.

Chapter 10: *Roots of Devotion*

In early June 1983, I was still cutting hair in the cramped basement of our rented townhouse. For the first time since Indiantown Gap, I was able to spend almost every day with my kids. I enjoyed the closeness, and I'm thankful for that bonding time with Anh. However, with a baby and four other children in constant orbit around me, my makeshift salon was inundated with all the accessories that came with them. Working from home was not a long-term solution. I needed more room to service more clients if my income was going to keep pace with the needs of my growing family—an Asian Brady Bunch whose number had just increased from six to seven.

A few months after Anh was born, I knew it was time to get a full-time job outside the house. After a fruitless week of driving around Northern Virginia looking for possible salon job, I had to take a break and come up with a real plan.

I prayed: Dear God, please guide me. Which way should I go? Then I patiently waited—not necessarily for an exact answer but for divine inspiration. When it finally came to me, the answer arrived in the name of a salon—one that, at the moment, existed only in my mind. It would be my own salon. All I had to do was find the right space and put my name on it.

The next afternoon when Chuong came home from work, I said, "Let's go."

He was confused. "Go where?" he asked.

"Let's go find someplace—any place, an apartment even. All I need is space for two chairs and a shampoo sink. I want to start my own business."

Chuong must have thought I had lost my mind. But he didn't ask any more questions. He just followed me to the car and drove.

After passing several shopping centers and apartment buildings, we spotted an apartment community called Woodlake Towers, which had what appeared to be some kind of retail space on the ground floor. We parked and got out for a closer look at the property located off Route 50 in Falls Church, Virginia, less than ten miles outside of D.C.

Peering in the darkened retail window, it was clear that the space was vacant. And better yet, it had obviously been a working salon not too long ago. It was rundown but came furnished with five chairs and a few shampoo sinks, which was all I needed to open my business.

It was the perfect location. The salon looked out onto a vast green space accented with well-tended flower beds, trees, and shrubs— a good place for my kids to play on days when they were restless and needed a break from being at Mom's side. And the salon and its hot pink marquee sign were visible from the main roadway.

I half-ran to the management office, with Chuong trying to keep up, to inquire about the rent. The manager told us the space was for sale, not for rent. We didn't have the money to buy the salon outright, but with equal parts curiosity and hope, I asked, "What would be the process and requirements to buy?"

Because he was eager to move a new business into the space, the manager agreed to let us rent-to-buy for just $500 a month. I don't know if I was more shocked by the low rate or by my ability to resist giving the manager a big hug and kiss.

Three days later, we signed the paperwork, and I was now the sole proprietor of my own salon.

At Beau Monde, I had learned the importance of entrepreneurship, networking, and having marketable skills. At La Madeleine, I learned the ins and outs of managing a salon, including diversifying services and branching out into product merchandising. I also learned to trust my instincts more and to trust others less. Now I was ready to be my own boss and to control my own destiny.

It struck me that I had just taken an enormous step forward as both a beautician and entrepreneur. What I had not yet realized was that I had also taken my first small step towards becoming a philanthropist. My business would eventually allow me to give something back—to repay a debt I felt I owed for the kindness others had shown me as I journeyed from Central Vietnam to Northern Virginia. So many angels had been there for my family and me—from Fox, to the beggar boy of Pleiku, to the many wonderful, giving friends I had made in America. I could never repay them all for what they had done for me, but I could pass their generosity on to others. It was my turn to give a helping hand to struggling families. It would not be very much at first, but it would be something.

Once my idea for a nonprofit had fully evolved—with valuable input and assistance from the men and women who came to me as clients but left as friends and mentors—my salon would become the source of another kind of beauty. I planned to help young children, one child at a time, as Mother Theresa had once said. But to nurture that kind of beauty, I still had plenty of work to do.

It was 1983. Fourth of July weekend was around the corner, and I was planning my own Independence Day celebration of sorts—the grand opening of my new salon, which I had named Beauty by Thai.

Thai is my maiden name. It's Vietnamese and was the name by which everyone knew me back then. I wanted customers to understand what they would be getting when they came to my salon and exactly who would be taking care of them.

On a Sunday afternoon in the Woodlake Towers party room, just down the hall from the salon, Beauty by Thai announced it was open for business. All night on Saturday, we swept, scrubbed, and mopped floors; we washed windows; we repositioned furniture; and we assembled, stocked, and decorated workstations to make the salon presentable. At 2:00 a.m., my stepdaughter Ann, who was now a young lady of fifteen, went home with me to prepare more than 300 spring rolls and other traditional Vietnamese food for the party.

The final detail was to change the salon's sign from the old name to the new one. It was the most gratifying task and also the easiest, since all I had to do was slide new lettering onto the building's marquee outside. Four months after the hostile takeover of La Madeleine, I was back in business.

The launch event was like a housewarming party—a celebration filled with friends, family, and clients, some of whom had followed me since my days as a beauty school student. Several Woodlake Towers residents also attended, probably out of simple curiosity and the promise of free food and drink. By retaining most of my old clients and gaining a potential new-client base within the Woodlake community, Beauty by Thai was able to hit the ground running. The salon was profitable before the leaves changed into their fall colors.

To celebrate the occasion, we bought our first new car, a van big enough to hold at least five kids. And now that we had a steadier income, we were also starting to think about moving out of our rented townhouse.

Making it even easier for me to consider a move was that I had already stashed away some emergency funds. Right after Anh was born, when I was still out of work and nervous about the future, I had reached out to my old friend Jerry. I told him I was not having any luck finding a job and thought starting my own business could be a solution. He agreed and, having just sold one of his companies, gave me a generous gift of $10,000 from the proceeds. Jerry told me to do whatever I needed to do with the money, so I put it into a savings account to keep as a safety net. But with Beauty by Thai's fast success and low rent, instead of using Jerry's gift for an emergency, we had the rare luxury of gaining quick access to funds for a down payment on a house.

Like the salon, our new home practically fell into our laps. A client came in one day for a manicure and gripe session. She was late and, after collapsing in my chair, began to tell me about needing to sell her house quickly. Her husband passed away the previous year, and she wanted a change of scenery.

Without missing a beat, while applying a fresh coat of brightly-colored enamel to her nails, I asked, "Can I see it?"
"Sure" she replied.

Later that day, Chuong and I toured the house. As we pulled up to the four-bedroom, two-bathroom rambler in Arlington, I was leaning out the window, taking it in brick by weathered brick. Ignoring the warm summer air, the hair on my neck and arms bristled. It was bigger than any house I had lived in since leaving Vietnam!

Inside, the narrow hallways, dark furniture, and deep brown curtains all but absorbed the natural light. It was possibly the saddest house I had ever seen—inside and out. I chose to ignore simple aesthetics, which could easily be refreshed. With a large backyard and a spacious, finished basement, I saw only the potential this house had for my family. More importantly, it was available, and at just under the asking price of $140,000, we could afford it.

We had found our home.

The owner's boyfriend, a licensed agent with Long & Foster Realty, prepared all the paperwork, making the sale even easier. Without consulting an agent and with only a three-page contract to sign, we bought the house three days later. The owner even threw in an upright Baldwin piano, which she decided was not worth the effort to move. None of us had ever played piano, but we happily accepted the out-of-tune instrument anyway. It was like we had walked away with a bonus prize from Wheel of Fortune.

As big as the house and its four bedrooms seemed, it was still challenging to make room for everyone. Ann and Bang slept in the basement. She took the bedroom while my son was perfectly content to curl up on the pullout couch, which he rarely even bothered to pull out. Karen and Mai shared a bedroom upstairs, and the baby—first Anh, born in 1983, later Elizabeth, who was born in 1985, and Kim in 1987—slept in the master bedroom with Chuong and me, usually in our bed. We had a crib, but after working long hours, sleeping in the same bed with my babies was often the only closeness I could enjoy with them all day.

The birth of Elizabeth was quite interesting. The salon was slow that afternoon so I decided to stop by a discount store nearby. I was already nine months pregnant and began experiencing back pains while at the store, so I returned to the shop early before my next client was to arrive. Mrs. Colby was a regular and arrived at five-thirty for her weekly Wednesday appointment. As I was blow-drying her hair I mentioned to her that I was having stomach pains and she declared, "Don't make me deliver your baby! Call your husband." I called Chuong around 6:00 p.m. and by 7:00 p.m., I was at the hospital and delivered Elizabeth by 9:00 p.m. Three days after I had Elizabeth (by Saturday), I was already back at work. I had originally planned to only spend three hours to make sure everything was running smoothly. I ended up working from 10:00 to 8:00 p.m. that day.

Kim was a baby that arrived by appointment. I was already past due, so the doctor had scheduled me to be induced. Because Kim was not born on her own terms and on her own time, this may be why coincidentally she now does not know when she will arrive with a decision about what she would like to do with her life. Because she did not have control of her arrival in birth, she does not want anyone to control her direction now, and I can understand that.

When we were able to sponsor my father's emigration from Vietnam in 1985, he moved into Ann's bedroom, and she moved upstairs into the space we had been using as a home office. We simply wedged a single bed in amidst the stacks of paper, books and boxes. A year later, my father moved out to live with my brother Phong.

In 1990 I sponsored my mother, two brothers' and my sister's relocation to the U.S., thanks to the help of two very good friends of mine, Leslie Gerson and Mary Marshall. Both were clients and both worked as general counsel for the State Department. With their background and intimate knowledge of the visa application and approval process, their guidance was essential.

Upon their arrival from Vietnam, my mother, sister, and two brothers also moved in with us. By then, Phong, my father, and college-bound Ann were gone, so it was easy to shuffle bodies and rotate rooms to accommodate everyone.

A full house meant more helping hands, both at home and at Beauty by Thai. My mom cooked and looked after the kids while my sister helped me at the salon. I encouraged my sister to get her cosmetology license. In the meantime, she could give manicures, which didn't require any formal certification. This allowed her to earn and save some money while working towards her own career. Within a couple of years, she got married and moved out.

While having my family around was tremendously helpful, the set-up didn't make everyone completely happy. Chuong and my family never got along very well. With an arrogance simmering just beneath his charming smile, Chuong considered them an imposition. Their presence in our home put him more on edge each day.

Even with his full-time job doing whatever it was he did for the phone company, Chuong volunteered from the very beginning to support me in building my business.

"Thai, you're very talented," he said. "So you should concentrate on taking care of clients, and I'll handle the books."

I was happy Chuong wanted to be involved with the business. It meant we could spend more time together. It also allowed me to focus on my strengths as a beautician, manager, and customer service specialist without having to worry about the financial details of the business, which only made my head spin. I was relieved. From then on I brought in the clients, made them happy, and made more money. I gave everything but my tips to Chuong.

As far as I knew, our division of responsibilities worked well for thirteen years. But as I would later discover, there's a major drawback to blindly handing over control of your money. Ignorance may be bliss, but bliss can come at a heavy price.

I felt like business was booming. It had to be; I was working so hard. But I didn't have a feel for exactly how much we were taking in or where it was all going each month. I did know one thing: we didn't seem to be enjoying any of the fruits of my labor.

Whenever I asked Chuong if we could take a family vacation, go out to eat or buy something (anything, really), he always said, "We can't afford it." We took short day trips and went to friends' houses for parties. But we mostly stayed at home and invited people over to visit. When I saved enough tip money, I would treat the kids to brunch or high tea at the Four Seasons in Georgetown. It seemed like going out for pho (Vietnamese noodle soup) after church was the closest thing to a vacation we could muster. It was beginning to feel like I was not in the driver's seat anymore.

When people asked Chuong what he did for a living, he would often deflect the question by saying, "My wife takes care of me." In social settings, self-deprecation was part of his charm. He was very good at hiding behind his smile and gift for conversation. He could fool anyone, including himself.

Chuong went full time with Bell Atlantic after we married. I was never sure exactly what he did there—something in sales or marketing. He never talked about his work, and I never knew how much money he made. But I guessed it was not as much as I brought in each month from the salon.

At times he seemed unhappy, maybe even embarrassed, that he had not finished college or landed the kind of high-paying job he felt he deserved. Before he could finish school, he got married and started having kids. I think he may have felt life had heaped one burden after another onto his shoulders.

Things had not been so miserable for Chuong in Vietnam. There he had help from his father, a well-known judge. He even went to law school in Saigon but dropped out, claiming his teachers were stupid. This was often his view of people with whom he disagreed. Despite giving up on school, he still managed to find a good executive-level job with a large company in Vietnam because he was smart, had family connections, and always knew the right things to say. But he had to leave that job behind after the war.

After we married, Chuong tried going back to school twice. He enrolled at George Mason University but dropped out again for the same reasons. He insisted he had more experience than his professors and knew more than they did about real-world business. He settled back into his old job with the telephone company and quietly grew bitter about his dead-end predicament.

I now understand what I didn't back then: Chuong was depressed. Maybe he was ashamed he had not fulfilled his promise to take care of his wife and children. Maybe he felt guilty for having taken me away from other men who could have provided more for us. And maybe he let himself become jealous of me when Beauty by Thai took off, and I became the family breadwinner. For a once-proud Asian businessman, this situation dealt a blow to his self-esteem and led him to make some very poor choices in a final attempt to salvage his pride.

Working six days a week in the company of the brilliant people who were my clients got me in the habit of asking questions. The majority of my clients were academic, business, and government leaders. While I styled and colored their hair, I was getting my own makeover— an unorthodox education. In a sense, my clients became my professors. They taught me about things I had missed out on in the classroom. Many of them also became my dear friends and remain important individuals in my life.

After months of immersion in this atmosphere, I no longer felt like I was going to work; I was attending a virtual institute of higher learning. Of course, I was not going to earn any degree. But that didn't matter. I was blessed with a unique curriculum that was teaching me valuable lessons in philosophy, psychology, organizational development, economics, entrepreneurship, political science, marketing, communication, community outreach, philanthropy and activism.

I was also learning that being successful often means associating myself with the right people and building a strong network. When I was not getting my fill of rich salon conversation with my impromptu professors, I was devouring the books they shared with me. Books like *The Prophet, People of the Lie, The Road Less Traveled* and *Jonathan Livingston Seagull* gave me new context for my journey from Vietnam to America and reinforced my spiritual foundation.

There are more ways to learn than getting a four-year university degree. This was what worked for me (and the non-existent tuition was very helpful). My salon became a free-idea exchange and hairstyling "think tank," where my desire to do something more for families and the community was given the intellectual fuel and guidance to express itself like never before.

I held daily brainstorming sessions with brilliant people like Pat

Sanders, who became Anh's godparent and was a National Science Foundation Fellow with a Ph.D. in math; Beverly Mattson, who had her Ph.D. in education and whose thesis was focused on children with autism; Emily Woo, who had a Ph.D. in economics; Bonnie Damron, who held a Ph.D. in psychology; Maryanne Datesman, an English professor; and Elizabeth Pan, with her Ph.D. in information systems. These women were already my professors, and now I was working with them on my own charity "thesis."

As we all put our heads together, an idea for a non-profit began to form. At first it was just a flicker that slowly began to materialize. But such things can take months, even years, of planning and refining, as well as money, to actually bring them to life. As the ideas were taking shape, I simply enjoyed the casual discovery process and nourishing conversation with my salon collaborators.

This social learning environment was opening up a completely new world to me. My salon started to feel more like Ancient Greece, where scholars would come together to discuss diverse ideas and opinions. It was a time of tremendous personal growth for me, but broadening my horizons was not the best tonic for my marriage.

Chuong seemed to be threatened by my friends, with their advanced degrees and money. When I began to question him, not just at work but also at home, passing along the concerns my friends had about why I was always working but could not ever afford to do anything, Chuong didn't handle it well. He was not as enamored by the Socratic Method as I was.

The more I questioned our finances, the more Chuong must have felt he was losing my respect and, thus, his control over our relationship. It was control he had been establishing methodically since before we even started dating. It began under the guise of being supportive, protective and loving.

"You should go to beauty school; you'd be great at it."

"Only a prostitute would marry a Caucasian."

"No one can take care of your kids like I can."

And then over the next two decades, so slowly that I barely noticed, he had tightened his grip.

"Why don't you just let me do the driving? It's not safe for you on these roads."

"We can't afford that."

"You handle the customers; I'll handle the books."

Ironically, Chuong had wanted me in a beauty salon to keep me insulated from the harsh outside world, supposedly filled with lustful men who might somehow take me away from him. It didn't occur to him that a group of smart, ambitious women would become a much greater threat to his authority.

Feeling threatened by the company I kept and increasingly overwhelmed by my questions, Chuong began looking for a way out— a way back to Vietnam, where he felt like he could regain some of his lost status, business success and self-confidence. I think he thought this would enable him to command respect and regain control.

In the spring of 1992, Chuong got the break he was waiting for. My friend Elizabeth Pan was looking to grow her business internationally. She needed someone who knew the Vietnamese market well. Chuong was an eager volunteer. He agreed to help her out and, at the same time, planned to improve his own situation.

Chuong said he would be able to tap into his old business network in Vietnam and begin building new relationships that could open up new opportunities for all of us. He came back from the initial scouting trip gushing about how Vietnam was the ideal place to earn big money and make all our dreams come true. But getting re-established there, he said, would take a lot of legwork. Although he still had a few contacts, most of his old network had fled the country or been lost in the war or re-education camps. He would need to make several trips back and forth. He assured me it was the only way and that the situation would be temporary.

Chuong traveled back and forth to Vietnam every few months for about a year after the first prospecting trip. Each time he would stay only a week or two. With expensive long-distance calls, poetry-filled letters, long goodbyes and elated hellos, he wanted me to believe that his family was important to him—that I was important to him.

Chuong's absence was challenging for me and the kids. Not only did we miss him, but we typically relied on him for nearly everything—managing our money, paying bills, grocery shopping, transportation (I drove myself to and from work, but he still handled all highway driving) and maintaining the house and yard. But I agreed his trips were important for helping us build a more secure future and assured him we could manage.

After that first year of occasional travel, he began to go more often and to stay for several weeks, even months, at a time. He insisted he wanted to see and stay connected to his kids, but I started to get the feeling that his only reason for coming home was to get more money— which I assumed was to help fuel his efforts in Vietnam. During each visit with us, he assured me things were on the verge of improving and that he needed just a little more time... and a little more cash. He promised he would be home for good very soon.

I tried to pretend it was no different than when I first moved to Virginia, when he was still commuting to and from New Jersey every week. I told myself this was just another business trip, even though this one seemed to have no end in sight. I was not happy with the arrangement, but I had no choice except to get used to it. I trusted Chuong when he said he would come back as soon as everything fell into place. Meanwhile, I had a business to run, and even though four of my children were out of the house, in college or married, I still had three young kids relying on me.

It was business as usual at Beauty by Thai for the next two years. It had to be, or I would have driven myself crazy worrying about what Chuong was doing. I could not let those old, familiar suspicions creep back into my head. I convinced myself that Chuong loved his family— that he was different.

Though my marriage was starting to stagnate, Beauty by Thai was thriving—at least if you measured success by the continued increase in customer traffic. I thought I had a pretty good handle on the business, and from what I could tell, it seemed to be doing just fine. But without Chuong's help or even a basic understanding of the salon's books, I was utterly lost when it came to gauging the actual state of our finances. I did, however, know what it felt like when money got tight. I thought the solution was to work harder and longer until the money situation improved, so that's what I did.

Working longer hours kept me away from my kids. The only consolation was that spending more time at the salon resulted in my building deeper connections with my customers. I tried to look at the situation as more of an opportunity than a burden. Every day successful people—women and men alike—came to Beauty by Thai in the middle or at the end of their busy days to enjoy a brief respite from teaching, conducting research, developing public policy, building legal arguments, running major organizations and creating financial empires. It was a gift to be in their presence. To accept it, all I had to do was listen.

With my clients, I shared personal stories that evoked laughter, wonder, admiration, outrage and tears. These people not only shared their knowledge; they also engaged me in conversation and wanted to know what I thought. On the other hand, Chuong seemed to become less and less interested in what I thought. I was discovering, day by day, that Chuong and I only shared the same circumstances, not the same passion. The growing distance between us was no longer just the result of his frequent travels.

Anyone who spent time in my salon knew me as a tough mom, encouraging my kids to study hard so they could go to college, something I was not able to do. Customers also knew me as a talented stylist with greater ambitions than just changing their looks. I also wanted to change the world.

In addition to talking about my own kids, who all had been separated from their fathers in one way or another, I often talked about my desire to help children whose parents could not or would not take care of them. I talked wistfully about starting an orphanage like the one I visited in Da Lat as a little girl. Alas, while my salon friends supported the idea of helping children, I could not afford the real estate, facility maintenance or payroll needed to run an orphanage, not to mention the cost of feeding, clothing, educating and providing healthcare for the children. It was just not a practical idea.

On and off, from 1993 to 1994, my friends and I batted a dozen similar ideas around the workstations, shampoo sinks and hairdryers of Beauty by Thai, as well as during other informal meetings at my home. By the summer of 1994, after months of research and deliberation, we settled on what we thought would be a more focused, attainable plan: informal fundraisers in my basement.

I found Emerson Lee's name in the back of a local Vietnamese-language newspaper in the spring of 1994 and knew it was fate. Emerson and I had attended La Cave Academy together almost twenty years before but studied vastly different subjects. While I had stumbled through a brief, unsatisfying career as an executive assistant, he had found immediate success as an accountant and started his own accounting and bookkeeping business. I called him the same day I saw his ad to get his help deciphering Beauty by Thai's books. As it turned out, he was able to do that and much more.

In addition to cleaning up the salon's books, he also helped (pro bono) with research that would enable me to set up my charity. In August 1994, I formed a limited-liability corporation called Devotion to Children in Poverty (the "in Poverty" would later be dropped) so that people could begin donating to an actual organization. It was my walk of a thousand miles beginning with a single step.

With so much going on in my personal life at the time, I didn't make much progress in the development of the organization, other than slowly recruiting board members. Devotion would not host its first fundraising event or accept donations until more than a year later. For now, discussions at the salon and occasional brainstorming over dinner with friends was about all I could manage.

In the fall of 1994, I received two pieces of bad news. The first was that Chuong was not coming back. On a call from Vietnam, he gave me an ultimatum: "If you want us to be together, you must move to Vietnam with the kids."

I thought he was just testing my commitment and loyalty to him, that this was one last attempt to assert control over me. I pushed back and upped the ante. "I can't move to Vietnam," I told him. "I've been there. I know how bad it is there still, and I'm not going to raise my kids there. It would be going backwards. If this is the way you feel, I want a divorce."

He responded without even pausing to take a breath, his words crackling across 5,000 miles of cold, twisted copper, "Fine. Have someone prepare the papers. I'll sign them."

There was a click and then a dial tone, and I was sobbing. I took maybe half an hour to compose myself before calling the only pro-bono lawyer I knew. Like most of my friends, he was a client.

Soon after, I received a second long-distance call bearing bad news. My father, who had since moved back to Vietnam, was very sick. He called to ask when I might be able to come see him. I told him I was not sure and asked if he could wait for me for a few months. I had to get through the holiday season—the salon's busiest, most-profitable time of year. I promised to visit right afterwards. Work was the only excuse I gave. I didn't see any reason to further upset him with news of a divorce that I still hoped would not happen.

༄

Chuong, the lawyer and I sat in the living room at our home in Arlington. Even as Chuong thumbed through the legal document before him, I hoped this was all just a bluff to get his way. It was not.

The lawyer told Chuong that once the papers were signed, our divorce would soon be final. Since he had been out of the country for several months, that time would count towards the legally required separation period. He used the word "abandoned."

As the lawyer relayed this information, I studied Chuong's facial expression and body language to see if they changed. They didn't.

Now that we were in the same room, I thought my husband would be happy to see me, or perhaps remorseful. No way would he be able to hide his true feelings like he could on the phone, with an ocean between us. I was sure he would back down. I tried to catch his gaze, but he purposely kept his eyes fixed on the document in his lap. He's still hiding something, I thought. I had known the feeling before. I don't know why I was not better prepared.

Chuong and I settled the details within thirty minutes. Because I trusted he would do the right thing for his children, I asked only that I keep the house and car and get custody of our children. In exchange, he pressed for me to assume sole responsibility for the mortgage and credit card debt. The latter, I assumed, would be no more than a few thousand dollars. I never used the card. How hard could it be to pay off?

I didn't ask questions, nor did I ask for child support, but I should have—on both accounts. I assumed my business was making good money and that because Chuong loved his children deeply, he would willingly contribute what was necessary without being obligated to do so by a piece of paper. That turned out to be a big mistake.

I don't need to explain what usually happens when one assumes such things (I wish I could go back in time and scream at the younger, shockingly naïve me). And I probably don't need to explain what happened as soon as I began to delve into the state of my personal and business finances with Emerson Lee. But I will.

As bad as I was hurting after meeting with Chuong and the lawyer, my meeting with Emerson made things even worse. Not only had my soon-to-be-ex-husband gutted our personal bank accounts; he had also run up balances totaling more than $60,000 on multiple credit cards and other lines of credit he somehow secured in both our names. He had also gotten a second mortgage I had not been aware of, something I would not discover until much later, when I tried to sell the house as part of my plan to reduce expenses and debt. My home was not the asset I thought it was. And most of the credit card debt was from high-interest cash advances he took out while in Vietnam.

To top it all off, he had also taken out a second mortgage on Beauty by Thai. I was at fault because at the time I was not able to read English well. I signed whatever was asked of me without fully understanding many of the documents. Where had all the money gone? No wonder he always insisted we could not afford anything. This definitely was not how a loving, responsible adult behaved. But I had trusted him. And I accepted some of the blame, because I let it happen.

These deceptions put everything I ever thought, knew or felt about Chuong into question. Who was this person? With every revelation about our financial mess, I continually asked myself, How could he do this to his children? He must have known the extent of his destruction as he sat across from me, signing our divorce papers.

It's hard enough when a spouse walks away from a marriage. Having him leave me with three young kids and a mountain of debt I knew nothing about was devastating. The shock and emotion resulting from our split and the financial damages would stick with me as a staggering reminder for many years to come.

My divorce was final on New Year's Eve 1994. I tried my best to see it as something that, although difficult, could also be a positive event—like a wildfire that consumes an aging forest, rejuvenating the landscape and making it lusher over time. Despite the heartbreak, lies and financial calamity that marked the end of my relationship with Chuong, good things came from it as well. Out of personal disaster, a greater purpose could now fully emerge.

Beauty by Thai was more than a job. It had become my way of supporting the community, supporting women and realizing my ultimate dream of helping children. Now I had to figure out how to move myself, my family, my business and my small organization forward, however slowly, despite the emotional burden and mounting debt I carried into the new year.

Chapter 11: *Long Way Home*

I could have, as Mr. Brick advised, "married rich." Instead, I fell in love with a man on welfare. I had ignored Mr. Brick's and Jerry's advice and turned down more than one opportunity to live an easier life. And for what?

Well, for love. When I look at my beautiful children, I am proud to say that they were all conceived with love. I loved their fathers. Sure, my family had not been on a vacation for seventeen years. I had no money to spare for leisure activities and hardly any free time. I worked six or seven days a week to pay the mortgage and salon lease, feed my kids and keep us out of donated clothing for a while. I had even gone back to work just three days after having a baby, because we were strapped for money. But as hard as things had been financially and as bad as things eventually turned out for Chuong and me, I had (and still have) no regrets.

I am also proud that I've been able to find ways to support my family ever since I first landed in America. I didn't have a rich husband to give me everything. Was I tempted? Yes, more than once. And sometimes at the end of a particularly trying day, I even caught myself thinking about how nice it would be to live a luxurious life with little responsibility—at least for a little while.

However, when I really thought about what I wanted for myself and my children, choosing the easiest route—marrying for money— was not for me. Maybe it would have led to the fairytale existence I had heard and dreamed about as a child. But for how long? To marry just for money alone would not have felt right.

I wanted to raise my children to respect themselves, value hard work and aspire to something greater than just pursuing material things. I wanted them to have loving relationships, happiness and fulfilling lives. I wanted (and still want) them to have it all.

When I came to the U.S., my kids were all I had. After Chuong, seven beautiful, well-educated children (including two stepchildren, whom I consider my own) gave me joy; a spacious home sheltered my entire family; and my business provided me the means and foundation for our future. In some ways, I suppose I owe part of my success to him. He always believed I could be a success. He was there when I needed loving guidance, which he gave so generously (if not always altruistically) for many years.

In the beginning, my relationship with Chuong was the stabilizing factor for my children and me . Although it took me a long time to acknowledge it, I had fallen in love with him. And his love for Bang, Mai and me was undeniable. Many suitors had come and gone, but Chuong endured. In the early years of our courtship and marriage, he showed me the love, admiration and respect I had hungered for since I was a child in Da Lat, fighting with my brothers to be included. Until those last few years, he took care of me, not advantage of me. Once our families came together, I really thought ours was a perfect union—not exactly a fairytale, but a story of humble beginnings and hard work that had every chance for a happy ending. These are some of the things about my marriage with Chuong that I have only recently come to understand. And I am thankful for those revelations.

On New Year's Day 1995, however, I was not as appreciative or idealistic. I was newly divorced and an emotional and financial wreck. Love and guidance would have been nice, but at the time, I really could have used some money. I had trusted Chuong to do the right thing for his kids. Instead, he turned his back on them. Because he had no legal obligations, he didn't contribute a dime to support his children after our divorce.

I went to his mother after we signed the divorce papers to see whether she might be able to talk some sense into her son. He had to realize this was morally wrong.

"You know, Mom," I said, calling her mom out of the love, respect and gratitude I felt for her. "I don't care if he doesn't love me anymore, but he left his children. What kind of person does that?" I now know the answer: one who feels defeated.

I should have known better. He had done the same thing to his second wife when he left Vietnam in the seventies. When we first met, Chuong was still married to her. She was living in Vietnam with his youngest daughter and thought they might join him and their older daughter once he set up a home and career in the States. That never happened. Then he met me. How could I have believed he would never do the same to our family? Maybe I had to share some of the blame, even as I lashed out at him.

Chuong's mother got very upset with me, probably because it was painful for her to hear me criticize her son. "You're not perfect either," was all she said.

"I know I'm not perfect, but I live up to my family responsibilities," I replied. "So should he."

After the divorce, Chuong told me I should go back on welfare to "solve your money problems." As if it was an easy thing to do, like applying for a library card, and as if the problems had been of my own making. When things got difficult, his solution was the same as it had always been—to walk away. After I had worked so hard for so long to earn respectability, after all I had sacrificed, there was no way I was going backwards. Accepting welfare again would have made me feel as though I had given up, just like he had, and that would have been a hard fall from which I might never have recovered.

Feeling the familiar burden of supporting my family, business, and fledgling charity, I started working even longer hours. This, I knew, was not a long-term solution. Unless I could slow the earth's rotation, there would never be more hours in the day. With help from Emerson Lee, I revived an idea I had considered at La Madeline— merchandising.

Beggars or Angels   Rosemary Tran Lauer

I had been curious for a long time about what it would be like to create my own line of beauty products. One day a promotional flyer for a cosmetics manufacturer came by mail to the salon, as if on the wings of an angel. I called the 800-number provided and requested more information by mail. I shared what the company sent me with Emerson and asked him what next steps I should take. He advised me to ask if I could come tour their cosmetics operation and learn more from their chemists about how they made their products.

For the next week, it was all I could talk about at work. What should I name my first product? How would it smell? What other kinds of products should I make? What would the bottles look like? Would anybody buy it? Which actress's hair would look the billowy best in slow motion for our television commercials? The possibilities were dizzying.

Within a few weeks, I had arranged to meet with the president and vice president of the pharmaceutical company to tour its factory and shampoo laboratory in New Jersey and discuss the manufacturing process. I took my stepdaughter Ann along since she had worked with me at the salon, had gotten her college degree and was interested in pursuing a career in the cosmetics industry. With her combination of beauty and intelligence, I hoped we might pursue this venture together.

After the tour, we sat down with some cosmetics chemists to learn about FDA-approved ingredients and how they tailored products to specifications. Two men in white lab coats explained characteristics of thickness, color and scent in the most technical terms. They talked about things like deionized water, surfactants, foam boosters, thickeners, conditioning agents, preservatives, modifiers and special additives.

As they started to tell me about the Cosmetic, Toiletry and Fragrance Association and the International Nomenclature of Cosmetic Ingredients, my mind wandered. I began concocting my own formula. I heard once about a shampoo originally designed for horses to keep their coats shiny and healthy. I interrupted the science lesson to ask if it would be possible to take the same formula and tweak it with FDA-approved elements for use on human hair.

"Sure," they said. "Why not?"

It was great news that I could take my horse shampoo and create a luxurious salon product for women. The bad news was that I would have to pay for a production run of at least 3,000 bottles, which was more than I could afford. But my visit to New Jersey had been fruitful. I got a good introduction to "shampoo mixology" and left, eager to pursue my venture.

Every year since I had graduated from beauty school, I attended a major beauty industry show in New York City. This time while there, I found a much more affordable manufacturer based in California to work on what had become my obsession. I learned I could have my product made there in smaller quantities and at a much more reasonable price. My unnamed shampoo was coming to life. But because it still needed funding, the project remained on hold.

A few months later, when Emerson gave me the complete picture of my personal and business finances, I decided it was now or never for my product line. If I could launch it by the holidays, the sales could help alleviate some of my financial problems and enable Devotion to Children to take off as well.

Sink or swim, I figured putting my energy into solving this dual funding crisis would be as good a way as any to keep my mind off my marriage woes.

*

"An engineer, architect, marketing manager and stylist walk into a shampoo-brainstorm session" sounds like the opening to a silly joke. But even though we were having great fun coming up with possible names for my new product line, my friends and I were very serious about Beauty by Thai's first exclusive product. As usual, we met at my house to talk things through over a glass or two of wine and a home-cooked Vietnamese meal.

I suggested we pick a one-word name, and my first choice was Desire. Although it was already trademarked, I still wanted it to be part of the product name somehow. I liked how the word connoted many different meanings, depending on who used it and when. So we brainstormed on two and three-word combinations: My One Desire (too limiting), Sweet Desire (maybe for dessert?), Burning Desire (not a great name for something meant to be applied to the scalp every day).

After a couple hours, it finally came to us: Secret Desire. The name had two useful meanings. First, it alluded to my secret desire to make money, not for myself but for my cause. Second, it appealed to women who didn't feel as attractive as they wanted to be—who secretly desired to be more beautiful, thinner or more confident.

"We all want to look and feel our best," I explained to the group. "But not all of us do. And probably none of us do all the time. What do you all think?"

It was late. We agreed to think on it individually and reconvene later at the salon to discuss our thoughts. I already knew what I thought.

The next day, as more friends and customers weighed in with their opinions, the only negative comment was, "It sounds nice, but seeing it written and thinking about logo designs, the acronym SD jumps out at me a little. It reminds me of STD—for sexually transmitted disease." Everyone laughed!

Since most of the comments were positive, we chose the name anyway. Secret Desire would be my cosmetic brand.

Having cleared that hurdle, I placed my first order for shampoo, conditioner and hairspray.

The Secret Desire line became an instant hit with Beauty by Thai customers. I spent $3,000 on the first shipment and sold everything for $6,000.

During the holidays, our "Free and Dry" hairspray even outsold Paul Mitchell's "Free and Shine" in our salon. I thought, *If I sell enough of this stuff, I'll be able to expand Secret Desire to include a full line of cosmetics.* But because I could barely pay for the first order, I knew it would be a while before I could place another.

As I prepared to travel to Vietnam to visit my father, I turned to Chuong for one last favor—an introduction to the Vietnamese market. If he could not offer financial support directly, I hoped he would at least help support my efforts to make money. Something I already knew about the Asian market was the not-so-secret desire among Asian women: the majority prefer to be fair-skinned—the lighter, the better.

Most of the cosmetics products available in the mid-nineties were developed for Western markets. In other words, the makeup was made for fairer skin tones. When Asian women used these products, the effect was not flattering. Because Asian skin tone has more yellow pigmentation, foundation created for Caucasians made Asian women's faces look whiter than their necks. They needed something that blended naturally. Secret Desire could fill that need.

Chuong agreed to help me. When I called to let him know I was coming to see my father in Da Lat in January, he said he could get my products displayed at a cosmetics trade show in Hanoi. There, he said, I would have the chance to talk to local marketing people and explore possible partnerships to help me break into the Vietnamese market.

On the first leg of my trip back to Vietnam—a flight from Washington, D.C. to New York—I met a married couple on the plane.

They were returning from what they called a successful business trip to the nation's capital. We talked a bit about the value of hard work, growing your business and the importance of being thankful for what you have. We seemed to be in tune with one another.

I thought I was making a possible business connection ... until I asked what he did for a living to become so successful. He looked around and then leaned over to me as if he was about to tell me a secret.

"I'm a dealer," he said.

"I did that once," I said. "But only for a few weeks before the police came and shut down the casino. I was not very good at it anyway."

"No, ma'am," he said. "I mean, I deal drugs—some marijuana but mostly crack cocaine."

Two things struck me when he uttered those words. First, I was impressed with the way this man could casually, honestly and intelligently speak about his criminal business and lifestyle. His personality and demeanor didn't match anything I had ever heard or seen on television about drug dealers. Second, regardless of how mild-mannered this man and his wife were, it frightened me to think that I had given them my business card, and they now knew where I worked.

"Oh ..." I said.

Our conversation ended soon after, but not before the dealer admitted he had often struggled with the fact that his business destroyed lives while providing him with a livelihood. He had been trying to get out for a long time but had become as dependent on the drug money to survive as his customers were on his product. "I've had enough. I've got enough money now, so I'm going to get out," he said. Then he added, "I'll pray for you."

It was a most unexpected ending to our bizarre encounter. Talking to this man reminded me of the beggar boy who roamed the alleyways and flashed unsuspecting shoppers in Pleiku. Like him, the dealer didn't know it was possible to live any other way. By sharing a little of my own story with a stranger on a plane, maybe I was able to show him it is never too late for a little hope, a little inspiration and a little education—wherever and in whatever form you can find it—to change your life for the better.

My trip to Vietnam was gut-wrenching from beginning to end. I went there with high hopes for growing my business and nonprofit. I also knew it would be my last chance to say goodbye to my father.

I arranged for my mother and sister to watch my kids and the salon while I was gone. Beauty by Thai had grown and settled into a nice rhythm, so I felt confident that it could hum along without me, at least for a few weeks. My anxiety had nothing to do with whom and what I was temporarily leaving behind in Virginia; it was about me wading into the flood of uncertainty, devastation and unresolved feelings Vietnam represented for me. All of these things hit me at once when I arrived in Hanoi for the cosmetics show, where Chuong had arranged for me to display Secret Desire.

Chuong came alone to pick me up at Hanoi's Noi Bai International Airport and take me to my hotel. We were cordial to each other. I expected to feel nervous and a little resentful, considering the way things had ended and the financial mess in which he had left me. But there was something in the way he still could not quite look me in the eye that made me suspect there was something else he was not sharing with me.

We agreed to meet later for dinner and then parted ways. When I arrived at the restaurant that evening, I discovered he had arrived before me and was already seated next to someone. It was a stranger— a woman.

After going through a similar experience two decades earlier, the pain was instinctive. My worst fear was confirmed a few weeks later when I learned they were not just acquaintances; they were together. Of all people, it was her husband who broke the news to me.

I had loved and trusted Chuong. And to repay my devotion, he had been unfaithful to me, just like Binh. Only this time it was worse.

Feelings I thought I had buried during my early years in D.C. came rushing back. A flash of memory left me almost in a daze—dinner with Binh's family the day I found out about his mistress. Then her showing up and everyone looking ashamed but not saying a word.

Now it was me who could not speak. I only nodded as Chuong stood and introduced me to her as Thuong—not "my ex-wife" or "the mother of my children." Instead I was barely acknowledged as an acquaintance. I suppose I might have been thankful I was spared the shock of meeting her by catching them in the act, as I had with Binh's mistress. I struggled to maintain my composure through dinner.

The cosmetics show became an afterthought. It almost did not matter to me when I realized, after just a few hours at the trade show, that my plan to sell Secret Desire in Vietnam would never work. I was not willing to sacrifice the time and money required for the constant travel back and forth or to make a habit of leaving my three youngest children—ages six, eight and ten—no matter how convinced I was that Vietnamese women would love my products.

As much as I longed to get away from Hanoi, Chuong and his new girlfriend, I wanted one last hour alone with him to say my final piece before I left for Da Lat. I wanted him to look me in the eye and tell me the truth. While we had been separated over the past year, I had suspected he might have someone else. He insisted I had invented her and that he had been wrongly accused. I wanted to have a heart-to-heart talk. Then a friendly goodbye. I didn't get it.

Chuong took me to the airport alone, but before we could start any meaningful conversation, the woman showed up. Today I can say with confidence that it was his loss. On that day, however, her callous message reverberated loud and clear: I have your husband.

I flew to Da Lat an emotional mess—my business aspirations defeated, most of my hair products (and the money I had spent to develop them) abandoned and my self-esteem the lowest it had been since I had failed as a secretary.

When I landed in Da Lat—feeling tense, emotional and exhausted—the sun was shining. The mist which draped itself daily across the wooded highlands had mostly burned off. It was the first time in almost twenty years I had walked these winding streets and seen the lush landscapes of my hometown. My senses became overwhelmed as I was again surrounded by its tiered hillsides and plentiful vegetable gardens, accented by glistening churches and waterfalls, with the fresh scent of pine cutting through wood smoke and clouded memories. Though much time had passed, the only noticeable change was the number of hotels and tourists there to take in the favorable weather and incredible scenery.

In stark contrast to the city's energy and postcard-worthy surroundings stood the home of my brothers, Chinh and Duong. With money my mother sent back to Vietnam, they had built it so that my father could live with them upon his return from America. She sent what money she could, but my mother could not go back to Vietnam for many reasons. Among them was the pain she was never quite ready to face.

The shanty was like an old townhouse on a narrow street in an aging neighborhood. I found my father lying in bed, which is where he spent most of his time. His small room was cold and damp.

"I waited for you, Thuong," he weakly greeted me as I entered his room.

I cried—as much for the perpetual squalor that my father and millions of Vietnamese still endured two decades after the war ended as for the knowledge that he was never going to get better. He had become depressed and began drinking heavily during his time in the U.S. He could not help dwelling on the status he felt he had lost since leaving Vietnam. When he returned to his home country, he was unable to regain the life he once knew. The lush gardens in which he had spent many hours tending his orchids and roses were gone—just one of many things destroyed by the war and resulting upheaval. He drank even more, and over time cirrhosis had consumed him. When his health failed, the relatively primitive Vietnamese healthcare system only accelerated his downward spiral.

I could not help but think of the better medical care he would have received in the U.S—including access to painkillers, the option of in-home nursing care, or at least a hospital room free of dirty, scurrying pests and the constant drone of flies over his bed.

Compared with most people in the area, my father was considered well off. At least he had a roof over his head and my brothers to care for him. But it still broke my heart to see him languishing in such horrible conditions. I knew then I could never have moved back to Vietnam like Chuong suggested. Just being there—seeing things I could not change and conditions I could not improve—made me feel frustrated and helpless. I no longer belonged there.

I did not want this memory to be my last with my father. During my childhood, we had developed a strong bond. We listened to classical music together, and I spent many hours with him in our rose gardens, watching him tend to the delicate blossoms. Whenever we were together, everything seemed at peace. Those were the quiet moments I wanted to remember, to hold on to.

In my brothers' home, I cared for my father as best as I could. I spared him the news of my recent divorce. I did not want to give him anything else to worry about. Just letting him know I was doing well with my business and that his grandchildren were healthy was the biggest comfort I could give him.

Saying goodbye to my father—the man who had supported my independence and encouraged me to strike out on my own as a teenager—was agonizing.

Saying goodbye to Vietnam was sad in a different way. It came much more easily.

A few weeks after I returned to the U.S. from Da Lat, my father passed away. He died in the house my brothers built to welcome him home to Vietnam.

PART III

TRANSFORMATION

Chapter 12: *Anguish, Beauty and Bliss*

The rainy season—Vietnam's dreary south monsoon—usually does not commence until May. I began to weep on the day I arrived in Da Lat in early February, and the downpour of tears lasted for six months.

If there was somewhere I felt at peace, it was either standing behind a salon chair, looking in the mirror and talking with a customer about the world, or coming home to laugh with my three youngest girls. But now my relationships with my stepchildren and also with Mai were strained because of the divorce. Bang was far away working for Morgan Stanley. And after seeing my now ex-husband with his new companion and after my father's death, it was difficult to find joy anywhere. I felt very alone and uncertain about my future.

Each morning I labored just to get out of bed. I was lethargic, irritable and distracted, but I had to keep going. In a very practical sense, two incomes had been cut to one. To run my business and be a mother, I had to work harder. Chuong's employee benefits no longer covered our healthcare. I told myself that no matter what I was feeling inside, my family, my salon and Devotion needed me now more than ever. I was overwhelmed. And no matter how much I worked, it never seemed to be enough.

Getting things done around the house was difficult. Chuong had always done most of the shopping, routine maintenance and yard work. Sometimes just thinking "that's something Chuong would have done" set me off. Even my younger kids—who were used to seeing me always busy, full of energy and generally put together—could tell I was not myself. They didn't understand why their mom was changing before their eyes. But they knew enough to give me space and focus on their schoolwork, if only to avoid being targeted for scolding.

In the same way life at home became uncomfortable, life at work also became strained. The business's books were a mystery to me. They had been Chuong's responsibility. I was emotional around clients and always on the verge of losing control. When it happened—and it seemed to happen daily—there was nowhere for me to hide. I could not run to my room, pull the covers up over my head and cry for hours, as I sometimes did at home. Often during those grueling six months, I would be cutting a client's hair, and she would innocently ask how Chuong was doing or where he was, or even how my kids were doing, and I would begin to cry hysterically. It's not easy to use sharp scissors near someone's head while gasping for air with eyes blurred by a slick of tears and mascara. Nor do most people appreciate a stylist who has to excuse herself two or three times to blow her nose.

I became critical and short-tempered with my staff. I lost clients. I thought I was close to losing my mind. For many weeks the depression was all-consuming, and it was hard to maintain a professional appearance. I had experienced the symptoms of depression before. And I had seen how they affected Chuong, how depression led to the poor decisions that destroyed his family. I did not have the money to see a therapist. I felt the answers had to come from somewhere within myself, not from someone else.

In the rare quiet times between work and home, a small voice kept reminding me that I had overcome hard times before on my own. I could do it again. I did not know exactly how or how long it might take. I just knew I must keep trying. My role as a parent demanded it.

While Beauty by Thai needed a smile back on the face of the business, my children needed their mother back—not the distracted, moping me, but a confident mother who could be there for them in body, mind and spirit. To be that person, I would have to take my feelings of hopelessness and turn them into something meaningful. I knew the best way to improve my outlook and channel my energy into something positive was to get Devotion to Children going.

I started by owning all of my circumstances and appreciating what I had, rather than lamenting what I had lost. I am a single mother and successful businesswoman, I told myself. I have seven children and a salon staff counting on me. Everyone, including me, has problems. Most are temporary. I am lucky to have friends who can help.

I cleared my head. It took six months, but I did it. During that time, I created a twelve-step program for coping with divorce to help myself and even to help others going through similar ordeals.

From there I was able to simplify everything else—money, home and work. Emerson Lee helped me get my financial house in order. Instead of finding ways to make more money at the salon, we focused on cutting costs and doing more with what we had.

With just four of us left in the house, we didn't need as much living space, and I didn't have the time or energy to maintain a house myself. I sold it in 1995 and moved the family into an apartment community a few miles away in Northern Virginia. Our new home was closer to my work and had good schools that were within easy walking distance for my kids.

I was talking one day at the salon with a longtime client—a photojournalist with *The Washington Post* who had just moved into Woodlake Tower—and was telling him about a war correspondent I met in Vietnam. As it turns out, my client had recently run into Fox. "You know, he's not in Tokyo anymore," my client said. "He's here now. You should get in touch with him!" He even gave me a number for Fox in New York.

Reconnecting with Fox was something I had meant to do ever since I started beauty school. When I first moved to Virginia, I had come across the slip of paper in my purse with Fox's contact information in Tokyo. Chuong and I were just friends then, and he helped me write a letter to Fox, letting him know I had made it safely to the U.S. Fox wrote back, but I did not read English well enough to keep up the correspondence. And I didn't think it was right to have Chuong continue taking dictation and translating for me.

Now I was single with three times as many kids as the last time Fox had seen me. I had a few reasons to consider reaching out to him again. One was that I still owed him a proper, in-person thank you for all he had done for me in Saigon. Another was that I had become a budding philanthropist and successful American businesswoman. I was proud of myself. So I thought it would be nice to reconnect with someone who knew me from my days in Vietnam and catch up with each other.

I called Fox's office and left a voicemail. He called back the next day to say he was coming to town soon for work and wanted to get together. I offered to pick him up at the airport, trying to impress him with the fact that not only was I speaking better English, but I could also drive a car—my own car.

"Great!" he said, sounding thankful, if not impressed.

It had been nearly twenty-five years since Fox and I first met in a crowded, Army-issued Jeep bound for Kon Tum. During that time, he had married, and then separated from, another journalist. He had become well known for his writing in *The New York Times* and other award-winning publications. He looked about the same—distinguished, with a little less hair. He said I looked the same too. I didn't think so, but it was almost funny how much I needed to hear it.

I drove into the Virginia suburbs to a Chinese restaurant a little more crowded and cleaner than the shack in downtown Pleiku where we had shared our first meal. Before jumping into our recent histories, we reminisced.

"Do you remember, once upon a time, when you called me a 'snob'?" I asked, opening the conversation. It took me several years of immersion in American culture to finally understand what Fox meant when he teased me as I tried telling him about my family's noble history.

"And I thanked you for it!"

"What? Did I actually say that?!" He was embarrassed but still laughed with me as I told him about the mistranslation.

"Why did you come back to Pleiku?" It was a question I had wanted to ask him for twenty-five years.

After staring for a moment at his plate of rice and vegetables, he smiled a sly smile and said, "Well, with the plentiful nightlife and culture there, how could an American tourist pass up the chance to go back?" Of course, we both knew he was kidding. Pleiku had none of that. It was not much more than a military outpost, an eyesore. The biggest thing happening there at night was the movement of troops and supplies, and even those were usually headed out of town.

This time I got the joke.

"You mean you really don't know?" he asked, sounding genuinely surprised. "I came back ... because of you."

With six simple words, he helped bury three years of self-loathing. He gave me something which, like our friendship, I could not define. I could only feel it and enjoy the moment. His words made me feel like someone deserving of love—something I had not felt since my divorce. Sitting there at dinner, a lifetime after Kon Tum, I knew that, however this relationship worked out, I would always treasure this moment.

"Thank you, Fox." We held each other's gazes for a moment, and then we ate, content to share fond memories of a night long ago.

After dinner, I took him to see my three-bedroom apartment in Falls Church. I was sure he would be impressed by how far I had come since Pleiku. He had seen me at my worst—my most desperate. Now I wanted to show him a more sophisticated me—me at my self-sufficient, English-speaking best. But seeing where I lived prompted an unexpected response from him.

"Well, it appears you left one hell hole in Pleiku and arrived in another," he said. "I'd like to take you away from all this."

He meant it as a joke, referring to the clutter and mess in the apartment. But his comment deflated me. Yes, it was just an apartment and not some fancy estate. But considering the places I had scraped and clawed my way up and out of to get to—and survive in—this country, a messy apartment larger than most homes in Pleiku, in a fairly-affluent Virginia suburb, was pretty good in my mind.

I attributed his failed attempt at humor to him just being nervous or tired. I didn't let it offend me—at least not after the initial sting wore off. Instead I filed it away for safe-keeping as another motivator and mentally thanked him for that too.

The night we reunited in America, we both said what needed saying. We understood each other. At the two most devastating times in my life, our spirits were connected. I am thankful that, for whatever reason, Fox was there for me. It was almost as if God had again sent an angel to help me at just the right time.

Fox and I met a few more times, spaced across several months. With each reunion, it seemed as though being together helped us rejuvenate each other with more positive energy. Our correspondence lasted another year or two while he remained in Boston and I in Virginia. We both had young children and other responsibilities, and our paths eventually led us separate ways.

I reach out to him now and again by e-mail or letter to let him know how my life has steadily improved since we last saw each other. I have not heard from him for more than a decade. I understand he has retired since we last connected, and I wish him well. I will always appreciate his kindness. Sometimes I wonder how two people from such different worlds could cross paths twice and how such chance encounters could develop into a meaningful friendship that I will treasure for the rest of my life.

꿈

We held the first formal Devotion to Children event in November 1996. When Elizabeth Pan asked what I wanted for my birthday, I told her, "Let's not make it about me. If you want to throw me a party, let's make it a Devotion fundraiser."

It was a relatively small-scale gathering. We printed formal invitations and held the fundraiser at Elizabeth's spacious home. I told my guests not to bring birthday gifts, not even a bottle of wine, but to bring their checkbooks instead. I would accept contributions in any amount—five, twenty a hundred dollars, whatever people could spare—as long as the checks were made out to Devotion to Children in Poverty.

The party was more a gathering of like-minded friends than a fundraiser. There was no caterer or live entertainment. About twenty big-hearted souls attended, and our donations swelled to more than $700. Devotion was growing!

Over the next year, I hosted similar small fundraising meals at my house. Sometimes everyone would dress up, sometimes not. Sometimes I would cook; sometimes it was potluck. But for every event, guests brought their caring spirits and generous offerings.

As we learned the fundraising game and devised more effective ways to appeal to prospective donors, we began to branch out from intimate dinner parties to larger gatherings. By the summer of 1997, we had raised enough money to rent a meeting hall in Georgetown and hire two professional tango dancers for an Argentina-themed event. I had attended a few tango classes with Emily Woo, who served on Devotion's Board of Directors at the time. We both had so much fun that we thought the idea would make a great fundraiser.

The tango event drew about fifty friends—and friends of friends—and raised more than $600. We still were not raising huge amounts of money, but we had successfully extended Devotion's formal event calendar beyond my birthday party. More importantly, we got a glimpse of our potential. This sparked ideas for all kinds of events and activities, most of which we knew were outside our budget. To get to that level of organization and maintain an annual lineup of unique fundraisers, we were going to need more time ... and more money. But we had raised enough money to hire a lawyer, which enabled us to apply for 501(c)3 nonprofit status. The journey was underway, and we were enjoying every minute of it.

The makeshift Devotion Board of Directors—which included me, Dr. Pat Sanders, Dr. Beverly Mattson, Arlene Heinzman, Dr. Emily Woo, Dr. C.C. Lee and Maryanne Datesman—met on and off throughout 1997. While simultaneously pursuing a nonprofit designation for Devotion, we explored different potential recipients for our first donation.

Based largely on the recommendation of Beverly, who had experience working for national nonprofits, we focused our search on groups dedicated to the well-being of children from birth to six years old. Beverly felt strongly that early childhood development was the most critical, helpless and least-funded area of need. It took a few months of research and brief discussions squeezed here and there into my six-day workweeks for our group to finally settle on the Mount Vernon-Lee Child Development Center in Alexandria, Virginia.

My friend and client Arlene Heinzman, who was working towards her Ph.D. in organizational development, had recently joined the board. She helped write the business plan along with our new lawyer Raymond, who later bought Beauty by Thai and turned it into a law office.

Soon after Raymond helped Devotion to Children secure the 501(c)3 designation in early 1998, we made our first gift. The child development center was the proud beneficiary of $250. Our goal was to eventually raise $100,000 annually. It was a humble, yet energizing, beginning. We knew we had started something special. This first donation was the start of what I hoped would be a long, prosperous journey. We had begun a tradition of not only giving, but also encouraging people to care for children who were not their own.

I held on to Beauty by Thai until early 1998, when after nearly seventeen years in business, I sold it. The debt in which Chuong left me had effectively crippled my cash flow. So when Raymond made me an offer, I took it—no questions asked.

I was fortunate to have good experience and to have built a solid reputation in the beauty industry by that time, which made it easier for me to find new work. Within days I had a job at Master Touch—a high-end salon and spa in the Virginia suburbs. It proved the perfect opportunity to rehabilitate my nerves and bank account. Over the next several months, I began to get my life in order.

After a year of recharging and paying down my heap of debt, I was ready for yet another new beginning. In February 1999, Emerson Lee (my accountant), who knew I wanted to get back into business, came to me with what he thought was a great opportunity. It was one that was too good for the entrepreneur (and dreamer) in me to refuse.

In the affluent business district of Tysons Corner, Virginia, Emerson had found a salon for sale (coincidentally, it was called Lee Salon). The property required little, if any, remodeling. I would only need to change the salon's name and decor to suit my taste. The asking price of $65,000 was way out of my price range, but the owner was willing to let me make monthly installments in order to buy the salon. I was back in business.

Buying the salon was another step in a long series of moves to gain a fresh start after the divorce. The next was to legally change my first name from my Vietnamese family name, Thuong, to my Catholic baptized name, Rosemary—which I shared with my godmother, Rosa Maria. This time around, the salon's lease would be under the name Rosemary T.T. Tran. I kept Tran, Chuong's surname, for my children's sake, to help them maintain a bond with their father.

With my new name, I abandoned the Beauty by Thai brand. Maybe it was a mistake, since Beauty by Thai was already a popular, recognizable name. It was more important for me, however, to have no reminders—a clean break from the past, in every aspect of my life.

I thought about naming the salon Shangri La, to reflect the peace and harmony that had long eluded me and the kind of experience I wanted to provide my clients—a small slice of heaven on earth. But I worried too many people would miss the reference and instead went with a more literal name: Beauty and Bliss. I thought it effectively hinted at the calming satisfaction of Shangri La, as well as my former Beauty by Thai brand.

Beauty and Bliss took off quickly. Word traveled fast through my network, and many clients returned. In less than a year, I increased my staff from just five employees to twenty-one—including nine hairdressers, five nail technicians, two skincare specialists, two receptionists, two shampoo people and a masseuse. Although the salon was bringing in more money than Beauty by Thai ever had, I was now paying $10,000 each month for rent, so I was still working seven days a week just to keep the business above water. While my skills as a beautician were very good, I was not as effective a manager as I would have liked. I compensated with hard work.

There is a term—"Running to stand still." That is what it felt like I was doing every day. It reminded me of a time when I worked all week just to afford a babysitter and groceries. While I had come a long way in America, somehow life had not changed much. But now I had developed a much larger support network, and that would eventually make all the difference.

In late 1999, something happened that made my efforts to launch the new salon worthwhile. In fact, there is no question in my mind that this event gave meaning and perfect clarity to every previous event, every previous challenge I had overcome and every decision I had ever made, good and bad.

I met Bill Lauer.

On that day, I found true love and Devotion to Children found a true life force (cue the *Hallelujah Chorus*).

Like many of my clients, Pauline Thompson was also a friend. It was the holiday season, and while at the salon, Pauline was going on about a dinner party she was planning. She asked if I wanted to come. She knew I was single and wanted to get me back into the social scene. Pauline was a successful real estate broker, so I figured the occasion would be an excellent opportunity to network and promote my new salon with her friends, who were some of the wealthiest local business people. I needed to go despite my exhaustion after work.

Having gotten lost on the way to her party, I was one of the last guests to arrive. I assumed Pauline would be the only person I knew in attendance, so I hunted her down right away.

After winding through the crowd, I finally spotted her talking to an older, stocky blond gentleman wearing a name tag that read "Bill." They were deep in discussion, so I got my own nametag and decided to roam around until Pauline was free.

Within five minutes, two men in nametags approached me, politely complimented my appearance, and asked me to join them for a drink on the couch. I declined their offer.

The next guy who approached me was not wearing any tag at all. "Hi,

I'm Rosemary," I said. "Where's your name tag?"

"Oh, I don't need one," he replied. "I've already met the girl of my dreams."

I was curious … and naïve. "Wow, where is she?" I asked. "I'd like to meet this lucky woman."

"Well, I'm talking to her right now," he said, as a fox-in-the-henhouse grin curled across his face.

"You're very kind," I stated, fighting to save my own smile from collapse. For a few minutes, we (mostly he) exchanged basic occupational data. He worked at a big accounting firm and had a Ph.D. in something, from somewhere. Before I could interrupt and make an excuse to leave, one of his friends pulled him away, insisting, "You've got to come over here, so I can introduce you to this woman." *Lucky woman*, I thought, grateful to his friend for diverting his attention from me.

I eventually realized this was not the innocent business event I had expected. It was a holiday mixer, and Pauline was trying to set me and all her other single friends and colleagues up with dates. While it was a kind gesture, I felt self-conscious and a little awkward. I had fended off many unwanted offers in the past from predatory men on the street and heard one too many say, "Hey, baby. Come be my mistress, and I'll take care of you." That's the last thing I wanted to deal with after a long workday. I thought, *If I can get out of here without some man's cologne on me, it will be some kind of holiday miracle.*

Just then the gentleman who'd been talking to Pauline when I arrived walked over to where I was trying to use a potted ficus tree for cover as I plotted the timing of my escape. Now with a better look at him, I could see he was just a few inches taller than me, but the confidence with which he carried himself made him seem much taller. His full head of blond hair was carefully parted. The kindness in his face was matched by a welcoming, almost gravelly voice.

"Can I get you something to drink?" he asked. Like the hair on his head, his blue eyes glimmered in the low evening light. His voice was confident but warm, businesslike but not trying too hard to make an impression.

More at ease now, I asked for a glass of wine. When he returned, he introduced himself as Bill Lauer. I soon learned that he was a real estate developer. This interested me because, when I was still in Vietnam, there was no comparable term for "real estate developer" in Vietnamese. If you wanted to build something, you didn't need permits or a plan; you just built it. I thought he meant he developed software for the real estate industry.

I told him I owned a salon and asked who cut his hair. He said Kudret, a master stylist and local celebrity of sorts, was the only one allowed to cut his hair. This was a turnoff. I thought, *How could he be so closed off to new experiences, especially one that would bring me new business?* Undeterred, I asked whether he had ever tried a manicure or pedicure. No, he "clipped" his own nails. Surely he had gotten a massage before? No, he didn't like anyone touching his body. Whatever salon service I offered up, he shot it down. And because I didn't know anything about software or computers, I figured there was nothing left for us to talk about.

Our conversation started with promise, but now I was just wasting my time and his. As I was saying goodbye, I asked what he did as a hobby when he was not developing software. I don't know why I threw out that last question—maybe because he had not shared much personal information and I was just curious. Looking confused, he smiled and said, "Exhaustion."

I didn't get it. Moving on, and almost to the front door now, I told him I had recently started a nonprofit to help disadvantaged children. Devotion to Children, I told him, was what I did for fun and relaxation, and we were looking for new ways to raise money.

His eyebrows went up. Energy was restored. Now with a passionate spark in his voice, he said, "Oh, that's interesting. I actually help raise a lot of money for local nonprofits."

That piqued my interest. "Would you help me raise some money for Devotion?" I asked. "I'm a fundraising novice. Maybe we could have lunch sometime to talk about it."

He agreed, gave me his business card and walked me to my car.

As the months went by, my business and personal finances improved. I moved the family out of the apartment (or "hell hole," as Fox had dubbed it) and into a townhouse, with help from Bang, who gave me the down payment. But because I spent most of my time at the salon, Devotion still just crept along with a potluck dinner here and a small donation there. I needed relief, and Devotion needed a boost.

What Devotion needed, almost as much as donors, was fresh thinking from someone with the right experience and business connections. Our next board meeting was coming up, and fundraising would be the main topic, as usual. Remembering what I had discussed with the stocky, blond gentleman at Pauline's party, I dug up the business card for William Lauer and gave him a call.

First, I dialed his cell phone. It was disconnected. Having your service cut off was never a good sign. *Could he not afford to pay his bill?* I wondered. Then I dialed his office number and was surprised to get his home answering machine instead of a receptionist. This guy must be a fake—a one-man show. Did he bring up this big fundraising operation just to impress me?

What could I do? I had already told my board that I'd made a solid connection with an important businessman who owned a house big enough for Devotion to hold a fundraiser in its foyer. To be polite, and with nothing to lose, I left a message and my work number.

Later that week, towards the end of the day, my salon receptionist gave me a message from "a guy—a lawyer named Bill." He wanted me to call back.

My lawyer's name isn't Bill, I thought. *Why does some strange lawyer want to talk to me?* If I had known that my receptionist had mistaken the mystery caller's last name, Lauer, for "lawyer," and that Bill was short for William (the name on the business card I had tucked into my purse months before), I might not have embarrassed myself after Bill answered the phone and said cheerfully, "How's the weather there?"

I knew a sales rep from San Diego who sold me pens, notepads and other branded items for my business, and this was the same question he always asked when he called. I was tired and cranky and didn't need any supplies from him.

"The weather here's just fine," I said, irritably. "What do you want?"

Bill, no longer sounding jovial, replied, "I thought you called me."

"What? When did I call you?" I asked, still thinking this was a sales rep wasting my time.

"Well, you left me a message." Now it was his turn to sound annoyed. "This is Bill Lauer. Did you want to discuss your fundraising?"

I was mortified.

Bill explained he was calling from the beach, hence the reason for his greeting. After I explained the mix-up with my receptionist, he agreed to meet with me again.

Because lunch hour was a busy time at the salon, we agreed to meet for dinner the following week. Bill offered to pick me up, but rather than have him come to my house, I told him to meet me at the salon.

He pulled into the Beauty and Bliss parking lot that fateful evening in a white Trans Am, wearing an equally white pair of high-water Dockers slacks and casual polo shirt. With his wind-swept hair feathered across his tanned, smiling face, he didn't look like the sophisticated president of a company. He looked like a preppy high-schooler on his way to the beach in the cheesy muscle car his parents bought him for graduation.

Bill took me to a very old-school Italian restaurant up the street, known for its roving opera singers and dated interior. Once we were seated, I got down to business. Trying to ignore the piercing baritone of a waiter behind me, I launched into a discussion about Devotion.

Bill asked about my ideas for growing my organization and whether there was a formal business plan. I told him we had written a basic business plan to help secure our nonprofit status but had not really made a concerted effort to follow it. We just did what we could in our spare time to raise as much as possible, and then the board kicked around ideas about where we should donate the money. My only long-term plan, I told him, was to raise enough money to start an orphanage or similar shelter for disadvantaged children, though we were still miles away from achieving that dream. We were lucky to raise even $500, much less enough to buy and manage an entire facility.

Bill shook his head at this and every other idea I shared, saying things like, "I don't think that's feasible in this market."

My English had improved over the years, but I thought maybe I was not expressing myself well enough. I got frustrated. *This business dinner is already a disaster!* I thought.

Bill seemed to realize this and smoothly guided our conversation to another topic: himself. He told me his life story, which included a divorce and two children—Kim and Andy. Kim was also a single mother, he told me, so he could only begin to understand how difficult it must have been for me to raise my kids alone since my divorce. This was truly touching. While he could be a bit abrupt when it came to business, I admired his honesty, openness and compassion. He didn't necessarily agree with some of my ideas for Devotion, but he understood me. And instead of trying to understand him, at least at the start, I had done something I promised myself I would try not to do: I had prejudged him. Once again, I was wrong.

Because I had requested the meeting, I offered to pay for the meal. Bill quickly waved me off and insisted on picking up the check.

"You can pay next time," he said, perhaps knowing I would insist on returning the favor.

If I had paid for dinner, one where we had agreed on almost nothing, there probably would not have been a reason for us to meet again. I would have to go back to my board and say, "I guess we need to look for another house."

Obligating me to pay "next time" was Bill's way of giving me—and us—another chance.

For my follow-up meeting with Bill, I made the reservation myself. We met at a different Italian place, just across the street from the salon. It was, in my opinion, a more appropriate, business-like atmosphere for discussing fundraising. Shortly after we sat down, Bill saw someone he knew walk into the restaurant. He said the man was a very wealthy businessman and a friend and asked if I would please excuse him long enough to go over and say hello. We were there to talk about fundraising, so if Bill needed time to talk with someone who might one day help my cause, I was not going to protest.

Bill returned to our table several minutes later, and we ordered. Over dinner he proceeded to tell me all about this friend. As interesting as the exploits of this rich stranger may have been, his story foiled my plans for discussing Devotion's needs. I mean, I didn't want to be rude.

Maybe feeling a bit guilty about having dominated the conversation with talk of his friend, Bill again paid for the meal.

"Please, it's not a big deal," he insisted when I reminded him this was supposed to be my turn.

"Give me another chance to make it up to you," I said. "Besides, we still haven't gotten to talk about what Devotion does or how we could use your help."

For our next dinner meeting, we went to Serbian Crown, an upscale Russian place in Great Falls, Virginia. Like the setting for our first meeting, the interior was very traditional, with lots of plants and classic Russian paintings. Rather than the obnoxious bellow of Italian opera, tableside musicians here played violins, underscored by the soothing lilt of accordions. The menus, printed in curly flourishes of calligraphy, did not list prices. It was the kind of restaurant I had only heard about in fantastic stories from my father. I told myself, Thank God I brought my American Express.

Then there was the vodka—in all colors and flavors. I had heard about Serbian Crown's reputation for having the best quality and selection around, but I had never actually tasted vodka in my life. When Bill offered me some of the spirit in a small, etched tasting glass, I played it cool and enthusiastically accepted. I didn't know the effect vodka could have—even such a small glass. I assumed it was like wine and that a few little sips would loosen things up and help the ideas flow.

The wonder and enjoyment of the whole experience overloaded my senses and clouded my focus. The food, music, conversation and vodka swept me away—especially the vodka. And again, we talked very little about Devotion.

At the end of the night, I was feeling warm, glamorous and proud as I waited, company AmEx in hand, for the check to arrive. But for the third time, Bill intercepted it.

I had heard several definitions of dating from my American friends. One was that if you sleep with someone, you're dating him. Another was if you go out with someone and he pays, it's considered a date (by that logic, I had been dating both men and women). Another was if you've gone out with someone three times, then you're officially dating. A fourth definition went like this: if you go out with someone three times and he pays, then you're dating, and he'll expect something in return.

Because of these dating guidelines, I always made a point to be clear with any man who took me out to dinner intending to date me. Before placing our drink orders, I would say, "If we're just friends, we can split the bill or take turns. If this is a date, you need to pay all the way. And just to be clear, I don't do sex."

Call me a prude. Call me presumptuous. Call me whatever you like. I call it a preemptive strike. As a cautious woman, I defined boundaries and did my best to avoid misunderstandings. I had found I needed to be particularly forward with Caucasians, who tended to be more aggressive than Asian men.

As Bill paid for dinner a third time, a tremor of panic moved through me. There had been no opportunity for me to present the rules, because I had not considered the possibility we were on a date. I was just trying to talk business. All I wanted was to use his house for the next Devotion fundraiser. Now here we were, apparently three dates in, and he was bound to want something more from me.

"Bill," I whispered. "We're not dating, are we?"

"Oh, yes," he said proudly. "We're dating."

I didn't know what to say. I tried to come up with some way to backtrack and reset things. If only this was our first meeting and I could establish "Rosemary's Rules of Courtship." Thankfully, before I could make my awkward plea, Bill put me at ease by saying, "But there's no expectations. I just think you're very nice, and I'd like to date you and get to know you better."

Crisis averted. It was a huge relief. Rather than adding pressure and complexity to my life, Bill wanted to take away some of both.

૭

Bill and I started dating in 2000. Being with someone who had a caring spirit, sense of humor and honest character was very important to me. And I knew Bill was a good person in all these ways. But my marriage with Chuong taught me that having a shared passion, whatever it may be, is essential for any romantic relationship to last. Physical attraction comes, and eventually it goes (gravity always wins). But shared passions endure.

Bill and I quickly bonded over our common desire to not only improve the lives of children and their families, but to also improve their chance for success throughout their lifetimes.

As we spent more time together, my attraction to Bill grew—intellectually, emotionally, spiritually and physically. It took some time, but I eventually allowed myself to think that maybe I had found my true love.

Before Bill, Devotion was limping along without a well-defined direction. The board members and our generous circle of friends did our best to raise money. But our efforts were piecemeal, often interrupted by our lack of solid organization and my backbreaking work schedule. Month after month, we pinched pennies and donated what amounted to loose change, which barely made a noticeable impact on even the small local organizations we supported, like the Thao Dan Sheet Children's Care Project, Alexandria Community Network Preschool and the Falls Church-McLean Children's Center. But these organizations enthusiastically received and greatly appreciated our donations just the same.

With Bill's help, Devotion picked up its stride, and its vision became clear. His disciplined thinking and strategic guidance helped the organization gradually begin to thrive, gaining more visibility within the business and nonprofit communities in Washington, D.C.

Devotion brought me to Bill, quite literally. If not for my off-handed comment just before leaving Pauline's dinner party, we may never have found common ground or a reason to see each other ever again. After all, the man had refused what would have been a free haircut. And returning the favor, Bill helped Devotion take off. Without him, I'm certain the organization would have shut down long ago. Yes, everything happens for a reason!

Bill told me he loved me for the first time in September of 2000, which effectively took our relationship to a new level. The buildup to this big moment proceeded in the clumsy-but-endearing way that was his trademark.

For his first attempt, Bill took me out to dinner. During our ride to the restaurant, he commented on a song that played on the radio, telling me how much he liked it. When I asked what it was about, he explained that it was about a man wanting to take a woman home that night.

"Oh, okay. That's nice," I said, missing his point.

For our next dinner out, the setting was more romantic. We were heading west into a gorgeous sunset and to dinner at one of our favorite restaurants, a place called Tuscarora Mill in Leesburg, Virginia.

Bill put a CD into his car stereo and skipped ahead to a particular track. As Chris Isaak's *Wicked Game* belted from the surround-sound speakers, he assured me, "You'll like this—this is good." Apparently it had been a hit in the late eighties and early nineties, but being a bit sheltered and ignorant of most American pop music back then, I was unfamiliar with both Isaak and his song. As the song faded out, Bill said, "I really like that song," hoping this time I had understood the meaning of the lyrics.

I had been looking out the window, enjoying the scenery and listening more to the music than the words as the song played. Even if I had been paying close attention, I don't know if I could have gotten the message. The singer's voice went from very high to low pitch, and he seemed to mumble during most of the song.

"What was it they were singing about?" I asked. So Bill quoted me some of the lyrics:

> *It's strange what desire will make foolish people do.*
> *I'd never dreamed that I'd love somebody like you.*

"Oh, that's very nice," I said with a nod and a smile, trying to show my appreciation for the song. But I still didn't get it.

With the wind again taken out of his sails, Bill made no more attempts to lay the L-word on me for the rest of the evening. But he would find success a few days later at a Sheraton Hotel bar. That night, as soon as we had our drinks, he announced, "I've been trying for the past week to tell you I think I'm falling in love with you."

It took a few seconds for his words to register with me. In that brief time, instinct kicked in, and without thinking I muttered, "Thank you." I realized this would not be well received the instant it left my lips, so I quickly added, "I think I love you too."

Not perfect, not romantic, but now officially on the record. We loved each other. After finishing our wine, we went home and kissed each other goodnight.

With Devotion expanding, I was extremely motivated to spend more time raising awareness and funds for the organization. For the first time in six years, I was satisfied with both my career and my personal relationships. I had finally met someone who loved and respected me as much as I did him. Anh, Elizabeth and Kim were healthy, happy and doing well in school. On the surface, my life seemed to be falling into place. Was this my happily-ever-after? In many respects, that's exactly what it felt like.

On the other hand, building my nonprofit while working seventy-plus hours a week to grow my salon business was beginning to take a toll on me. I didn't see my family or Bill nearly enough for my or their liking. Even when I was with them, it was not always what I would call quality time. I was constantly tired, stressed, irritable or all of the above. Bill suggested it might be time for me to slow things down. I agreed. After all, why not try something new?

I sold Beauty and Bliss in December 2000 to a hairdresser who had been asking to buy me out and returned to Master Touch as a stylist. The transition allowed me to spend more time with Bill, which enabled our relationship to grow. I could now spend more time with my kids. And my energy levels and overall health began to recover almost immediately.

But things were about to change again.

One day a long-time client named Susan came into the salon and asked me to cut her hair very short. Such an odd request from a woman with a glorious head of hair prompted me to ask why she wanted to drastically change her look.

"It's all going to fall out anyway," she said. "I have breast cancer, and I'll be going through chemo soon."

Her admission shocked me. I don't know what struck me the most—

the way she said it so casually or the fact she was only in her early forties. Susan was beautiful and in excellent shape. If she had not told me about it, I would never have guessed she was battling for her life.

I had lost other friends and clients to cancer, including my dear friend Stephanie Cole, who was in her early forties when she died. But it was not until Susan shared her story, including the fact that she found the lump during a self-examination that I thought about examining myself.

Chapter 13: *Rejuvenation*

I found the lump in my right breast in February 2001. Unlike many survivors, I do not remember everything about the day I discovered that I had cancer. But I do remember that I was alone. Bill was out of town. My daughters were in New York visiting Bang. I had stayed home to supervise the workers who were replacing the worn carpet in our townhouse with hardwood floors. After the sale of Beauty and Bliss a few months earlier, giving my home a long overdue facelift was a small luxury I could finally afford. I had sent the kids away and asked Bill, who was at the beach, if I could stay at his house for a few days during my renovations.

I had been giving more thought to the unusual conversation with my client Susan just a few days before. With some quiet time and space to myself, this was a good opportunity to follow her advice and perform a self-exam. It had been at least five years since my last mammogram, if not longer. But I lived a pretty healthy lifestyle and was still relatively young. My energy levels had improved since selling the salon, so I didn't feel an urgent need to get checked out.

I had never done a self-exam, but Susan had given me some pointers. After a few minutes standing in front of Bill's bathroom mirror with one arm raised and fingers slowly probing, I felt something. It was small and hard, like a dried pea.

I called Dr. Rimola, my gynecologist, the next morning to make an appointment. I felt better than I had in a long time and had no unusual symptoms, so I was not too worried. On the other hand, I definitely wanted an expert opinion.

A week later I was sitting on an exam room table, bathed in unflattering light, showing the doctor my right breast.

"This is where I felt it," I said, pointing to the spot.

He gently touched the area and quickly told me he thought it was not a big deal. "I would not worry," he said.

I was relieved. I had not really known whether I was doing the self-exam correctly. Maybe I had mistaken something normal for something serious.

Dr. Rimola asked how long it had been since my last mammogram. When I told him, he ordered one for me, "just to be sure."

I called that afternoon to schedule my mammogram, but the earliest-available appointment was not for three months. Waiting that long for a definitive answer would have driven me insane. I told the scheduler I had found a lump and that my doctor needed the test results as soon as possible. That detail scored me an appointment the next week. The tradeoff was I would have to go to a facility much farther away in Lansdowne, Virginia. It was about an hour's drive from D.C. and forty minutes from where I lived. But for peace of mind, it would be well worth the trip.

I drove to the appointment alone. After my last mammogram, I was told everything was fine and I could go home. This time the technician asked me to stay for a sonogram, after which I was told the doctor would like to see me.

I had come to the appointment with no fear. I was fairly young, I ate healthy and my gynecologist had said there was no problem. But now the doctor wanted to see me. *The doctor never asks to see you unless there's something wrong,* I thought. Now I began to worry.

The doctor got right to the point. He said that on a scale of one to five, with five being the highest level of suspicion for cancer, my lump was a level four. I would need a biopsy.

I knew about biopsies. I had heard about them from several friends, many of whom had been diagnosed with cancer. I was starting to shake a little, trying to fight back the fear. My first urge was to throw myself on his desk, sobbing, and ask, "What am I supposed to do now?" To keep my emotions in check, I tried to remain as rational as possible and turned my mind towards taking the most logical steps to overcome this, my latest setback.

"I am a single mother with three young daughters," I told him. "I need to ask you a very tough question. If I was your wife, which doctor would you recommend I see? Who is the best person for treating breast cancer?"

He thought for a moment, carefully considering my situation before answering, "I would send my wife to Dr. Franco. No question." As he jotted down Dr. Franco's contact information and handed it to me, he added, "But please don't worry. Nothing is certain until the biopsy results are in."

I thanked him and walked out of the building into the biting winter wind. It took me three tries with an unsteady hand to get my key into the car door. Sitting in the parking lot, I thought about my kids and wondered how I could tell them I was sick. It was already difficult to find a babysitter while I worked during the day. If I was suddenly completely out of commission, then what would I do with them? They had no father around—and maybe one day soon, no mother.

Fifteen minutes later, the car's windshield had completely clouded over. I wiped my eyes and turned the defroster on high so I could see my way home.

The morning after my mammogram, I called Bill. I needed to share the news with someone, and I was not ready to tell my kids—not until I was certain there was anything important to tell them. "I'm sorry, dear," he said, sounding as though he had gotten bad news himself. "What can I do?"

≈

When I called to schedule an appointment with Dr. Franco, I was told that he was nearing retirement and was not taking any new patients. "We might be able to squeeze you in, in June," his receptionist said. I could not wait that long. So I scheduled an appointment with someone else in the practice, figuring if I could not get the good doctor himself, someone with whom he chose to partner would be the next best thing.

I got nervous as soon as I saw Dr. Franco's fill-in, who appeared to have some kind of facial paralysis. His cheek and lip drooped on one side, as if he might have recently suffered a stroke, and a bit of saliva dangled from his mouth. I certainly did not want to insult the man, but this was my breast, and I didn't want to have any questions about the physical limitations of whoever would be wielding a scalpel over it. When I apologized and asked if he could refer me to another doctor, he said I could have the biopsy done robotically. That sounded like an excellent option to me.

The robotic biopsy turned out to be the easiest part of this ordeal. Afterwards I waited a week for the results, my anxiety building each day. I went to work every morning distracted, putting on a smile for my kids and customers. Anyone who has ever gone through similar tests knows and loathes this feeling—holding your breath while your mind races, unable to concentrate on even the simplest tasks, but having to function all the same. While you are eager to know the results, part of you doesn't want to hear them, instead wishing never to have known, never to have gone looking for something wrong in the first place, never to have felt a lump where other people—normal, healthy people— didn't. Part of you wants to have remained blissfully ignorant.

In addition to my fear of what the test results could mean for my future, there was also an underlying cultural influence that worried me. In the Vietnamese community, cancer still carries a social stigma. The stigma has mostly disappeared in the U.S. and other Western societies, as awareness and understanding have increased with the efforts of such organizations as the Susan G. Komen Foundation.

Many Asians afflicted by cancer or other serious health conditions worry that their problems might be the result of karma— a punishment for some transgression from an earlier life. Though this is an outrageous notion to most Westerners, it often plays on the minds of those subscribing to Buddhist philosophy. But while I do believe there may be consequences for what you do in this life, being punished for past lives—something you have no way of knowing about or controlling—is something I don't subscribe to.

Years later, while working at my current job, a Vietnamese client asked me about my experience with cancer. I don't know whether she was being cruel or just ignorant, but she had the nerve to ask, "Do you think you went through all that because of karma?" Her comment reminded me why I don't subscribe to the philosophy of karma and past lives, even though many other people still believe in it. In fact, this is part of the reason I converted to Christianity.

Many women also fear the severe physical effects that can accompany harsh cancer treatments—from losing their hair to the physical deformities caused by mastectomies and other surgical options. They worry about being undesirable once treatment is complete. Would others, especially prospective mates, think them weak or defective? Would they ever be loved again?

Over the next week, every time my home phone rang or the receptionist at Master Touch told me I had a call, my heart jumped a little. When the call finally came, I was at work. The hopeful part of me kept thinking, They only give good news over the phone. It took only a second for that hope to dim. Dr. Rimola wanted to see me in person.

When we sat down together, the doctor told me the test results had come back "positive." Treatment options needed to be discussed. I would need surgery—soon. Despite all my progressive thinking, I was suddenly overwhelmed with fear. Somewhere in the back of my mind and in the pit of my stomach, I felt the fear of rejection, of being considered weak or, worse, unlovable.

I put my fears aside for the moment. When I got home, I would need to call Dr. Franco's office with a clear head. I needed a good surgeon quickly. The only one who could perform the surgery right away was a doctor named Kodama. My previous gynecologist, Dr. Price, whom I had seen for many years, was precise, businesslike and very sensitive to Asian cultural standards. As an Asian woman, this meant a lot to me. If Dr. Kodama was anything like her, I would be in very good hands. The thought comforted me.

*

Dr. Kodama calmly walked me through everything I needed to know. I would need either a lumpectomy or mastectomy. He recommended a radical mastectomy for two reasons. First, the cancer that originated in the milk ducts—which were as intricate as a thousand spider webs—was extremely hard to remove completely with radiation. And if he didn't get it all, the cancer could come back and spread to other areas. Secondly, because I was a single mother with three children still in school, it was important to get all the cancer the first time so I could avoid a lengthy treatment with repeated visits. While I understood this rationale, I was still hesitant about having my entire breast removed.

Before surgery I would have to see three other specialists recommended by Dr. Kodama: a radiologist, oncologist and plastic surgeon. Since I still had a little more time to choose between the two surgical options, I decided to consult with the other specialists first.

During my visit with the radiologist, I asked what she would do if she were in my shoes. Would she do the lumpectomy and radiation or the more radical surgery? When she said it was an unfair question to ask her, I replied, "Unfortunately, it's the question I have to ask someone. And now

I'm asking you, as a woman and a doctor who knows much more than I do about these treatments."

"I don't think radiation would help," she conceded. With that answer, my choice was easy.

The radiologist Dr. Kodama and Dr. Victoria Suh, the plastic surgeon, all recommended what's known as the *transverse rectus abdominis myocutaneous* (TRAM) flap operation. The technique, as it was described to me, seemed to involve a lot of cutting and rearranging. It was a more complex procedure than simply getting an implant. For the TRAM flap, they would remove the breast and replace it with one made out of muscle, fat and skin from my lower abdomen or upper back. Because my profession required me to work with my arms raised most of the time, a TRAM flap was the better option for me.

Aside from providing better mobility and a more natural reconstruction than an implant, there were some other perks to the TRAM flap. I would be getting a tummy tuck for my trouble. Considering the time needed for that long, deep incision to heal and the excruciating pain that never seemed to let up, I'm not sure I would have chosen the procedure if I had known then what I know now.

We scheduled the operation for mid-June—just a few months after I found the lump. Everything seemed to happen quickly. In my haste to confirm my diagnosis and arrange for treatment, I had let two things slip my mind. First, I had not told anyone in my family about my condition. I had been avoiding it, at least until I knew the extent of it. Also, while I had prepared myself mentally for surgery and treatment, I had not prepared for what would happen if I didn't live through it. They called it a radical mastectomy for a reason.

Before my surgery date, I had two difficult tasks to confront: breaking the news to my kids and making out my will. Like many working-class people who struggle just to make ends meet, I thought writing a will was something only wealthy people had to worry about. But I still had three children under age eighteen at home relying on me, and I had to deal with these important things now.

※

The prospect of death had crossed my mind a few times earlier in my life—on the dock in Saigon, in the middle of the Pacific and on that one dark day during secretarial school. But this was the first time I felt the verdict of life or death was completely out of my hands. Even with shrapnel flying over my head on that oil tanker, at least I had the chance to duck.

In the past I had managed to survive by doing what I had to do to save my kids. They depended on my resourcefulness and my ability to reach deep inside myself for the strength to carry on. This time I had to place all my faith in God and my doctors. I was confident my older children would be able to take care of themselves, but their younger siblings who still lived with me would need more than faith to take care of them if I was gone. I had to plan for them.

Luckily, I had a friend and lawyer named John who could help on short notice. John gave me a piece of advice that allowed me to stay focused during those last weeks before surgery. As I began to lay out the whole picture of my assets, at least as much as I understood, and to explain how these things might be divided among my children, John put his hand on mine to stop me.

"Rosemary, please don't worry about the money," he said with the warmth of a minister visiting a grieving widow. "It probably won't be much, and it can easily be divided later. What you should worry about is who will take care of your kids."

It was surprising that my lawyer would have to remind me of something I had thought about nearly every waking moment since leaving Vietnam. Cancer is a word not many people handle with grace. And it was now echoing in my head, diverting my attention from what had been my life's mission.

John added, "Under the circumstances, you're taking all of this pretty well. How can you be so calm?"

As with most emergencies that had come my way, I had gone about solving this problem logically and by living completely in the present. Maybe I was still in denial. Maybe it was my mothering instinct—which had served me well during past crises—kicking in again.

"If I fall apart, then what would happen?" I asked him. "That would not help anyone."

I left the lawyer's office, went home and called Bill. He was a sensible businessman who could help if we needed to sell the house or help handle other business affairs. More importantly, he was a concerned and thoughtful man who could provide emotional support, as well as help keep me calm and see things more clearly.

I called Bang in New York. His wife had just given birth to their first child, and his job at Morgan Stanley kept him extremely busy. I told him I understood it might be difficult to get away, but I had something serious to discuss with him and his siblings. I needed him to come home for the weekend. Then I called Mai to make the same request. I went back to work the next day and tried to stay calm.

That weekend my children sat on our living room couch, looking at me with curiosity and anticipation. Having all of them gathered at home should have been reason to celebrate. Not that day.

My younger daughters, who had seen my behavior change over the past month, probably had some idea that bad news might be coming. But the rest knew nothing.

Bill was there by my side for support and to assure my kids that if they needed help with anything, he would be there for them too.

I took a deep breath. It was time to tell them.

"For the past few weeks, I've been facing something scary," I started. "It might have been nothing at all, so I didn't want to tell you about it until I knew more."

I paused, searching for the right way to continue.

The next words to come out of my mouth were the most difficult I ever had to express in any language: "I have cancer, and I'm going to have surgery. We need to plan in case I don't make it."

I felt like I was outside myself, listening to the words as they tripped over my lips and tumbled through the air. The only sound in the room was my voice. There were no gasps, no tears and no hugging or other displays of emotion. My children remained composed and respectful as they listened—an Asian cultural trademark they had learned despite having grown up in the U.S.

"I'm having surgery soon and asked you here today so we can talk about what happens after that. If I come out of it okay, that's great. But if I don't, I need to know that Anh, Elizabeth and Kim have someone to care for them."

As my words echoed through the townhouse, I looked into the eyes of my youngest daughters and tried not to let my voice shudder at the thought that I might be leaving them. I prayed they would not see the fear in my face. I wondered what was going on behind their eyes as they looked at one another, then back at me.

Kim, the youngest at twelve years old, broke the silence. "I guess I'll go live with Bang."

Bang nodded in agreement. "Of course, I will take care of Kim."

"I guess someone would take me in," said fourteen-year-old Elizabeth, as though she would rather not think too hard on the details just yet.

Finally, Anh—a junior in high school and the oldest still living with me—said, "I'll be going away to college in a year, but I could probably live with a friend until then if I had to."

Their responses surprised me. They were very calm and logical. Just like their mom, they may have been falling apart inside, but outwardly they remained composed. I was even prouder to hear their reactions when I asked what each of them would like to have of mine.

"I don't need anything, Mom," my son replied, nearly cutting off the question. "Save it for the girls."

He seemed to speak for the group. His sisters drove the point home, saying they just hoped everything would be okay and that I should not worry about them. They just wanted me to concentrate on myself. This is the most vivid memory I have from that day. I have appreciated and cherished it ever since.

I had surgery early on June 14, 2001. It was a Thursday. Bill drove my kids and me to the hospital. As an orderly wheeled me into surgery, I thought back to the day he first said he loved me. It was a definite turning point in our relationship—and in my life. That day at the hospital was yet another.

Before we parted at the operating room doors, he kissed me gently and said, "If I could, I would trade places with you."

After Drs. Kodama and Suh worked nearly six hours to rid my body of cancer and then put me back together, Bill's actions again proved to me—

more than any words or Chris Isaak song ever could—how much he truly loved me. Anh had driven herself and her sisters to school while I was in surgery, but Bill stayed, "because I love you." Showing love is always preferable, but letting the person hear it once in a while doesn't hurt. Bill's timing, on this occasion, was impeccable.

When I opened my eyes, Bill's was the first face I saw. It gave me an all-over warm feeling. The morphine probably helped, but I was definitely glad he was there. He asked me how I felt, and I told him, "I feel like a ten-ton truck has run me over repeatedly, and now it's parked on my chest." And I was not exaggerating.

I was in the hospital for the next five days. Family and friends occasionally stopped by, giving my spirit a big boost. Being alone in the hospital can be an extremely isolating, disheartening experience. The short-staffed nurses can only do so much, and it's not their job to keep patients entertained and feeling upbeat.

While other visitors came now and again, Bill was there every morning before work and again each evening. He would stay with me until visiting hours were over and he was asked to leave. Regardless of the time of day, my hair was always moist and matted and my eyes were half-shut and crusted over. He would brush the hair from my face, adjust my pillow, call for a nurse, hold my cup of water and bend the straw so I could drink—none of which I could do for myself without excruciating pain slicing through my abdomen and chest. I mostly tried to lie completely still. But even the smallest movements, like talking or drawing a shallow breath, sent searing pain from my shoulders to my pelvis.

I was cut from hip to hip and then from my right armpit to my sternum. The doctors had peeled back skin in order to clean everything out—everything, including my right breast—and then moved a portion of skin, muscle and fat up from my left side to reform and graft it where my breast had been. To close the football-shaped gap left behind, they stretched the skin upwards and stitched it together. Post-op, I had not one but two enormous wounds that would require constant drainage and months to heal. Until then it felt as though every movement threatened to rip me apart at my seams.

On day three of my stay, I was strongly encouraged to get up and try to walk to the bathroom. Like after giving birth, it's one of the first requirements for being allowed to go home. After failing to find a nurse, Bill was courageous enough to help me inch myself to the edge of the bed and slowly slide down until my feet found the floor. Once I felt steady enough, I tried to stand upright but could not.

I gingerly shuffled the ten feet to the bathroom—hunchbacked, whimpering and clutching the rolling IV pole on one side, with Bill on the other to steady me. Each deliberate step caused my newly-mended muscles to contract and stitches to burn. If not for the fact that all my focus was on the pain and making it to the bathroom in time, I would have been mortified about the view Bill had of my mostly uncovered posterior, bedsores and all.

Once inside the bathroom, I gripped the tiny sink for balance and closed the door behind me. I wanted to assess my situation in private. At barely five feet tall, I could not see my whole self in the bathroom mirror—which was probably a blessing. I could only see my body from the neck up, and that was not pretty. My eyes were still swollen, skin blotchy, brow sweaty and lunatic hair busted free of its Secret Desire aerosol bonds. I had to guess about the parts of me I could not see, but I knew certain parts were gone. I felt like half a woman. In just a few days, I had changed from a vivacious salon professional into a beautician's nightmare. Now the burning was in my eyes, as they welled up with tears of disbelief.

I was relieved to see that Bill was still there when I opened the door. If we had been husband and wife, his dedication would have been expected. But we had only been serious for a few months, so I would not have blamed him if he had bolted as soon as I disappeared into the bathroom. Seeing his smiling face as he reached to support me on the return trip to my bed made me love him more than I have ever loved anyone other than my children.

"Do I look horrible?" I asked, wanting to hide my face.

"I think you still look cute," he said, with all the diplomacy, sincerity and blind optimism of someone either head-over-heels in love or up for re-election. I tried not to laugh and ended up crying again— not because of my appearance anymore, but because of the way Bill took those feelings of vanity and embarrassment away. I was not used to having someone care and love me as I am, with all of my flaws and imperfections.

Bill brought me home from the hospital on Sunday. Climbing the stairs to my townhouse and then up to my room on the second floor, I might as well have been scaling Mount Everest. He helped me ease into bed, where I would remain for the next uncomfortable week, except to use the bathroom.

My kids brought me food. Anh (God bless her) was my head nurse. She helped keep me on schedule with medications. And twice a day, she emptied the drainage bags attached to the catheters that stabbed at my sides whenever I tried shifting positions. Bill and Elizabeth Pan also seemed to be around whenever I needed their help— to provide rides to appointments as well as much-needed company. For the first week, however, I mostly used medication and sleep to escape the pain.

By the end of the week, Bill was exhausted from working and spending the rest of his time helping my family and me. He decided to retreat to his beach house for the weekend to recharge. He had certainly earned at least that. Unfortunately, I did not see it that way at the time.

I thought when he said he loved me that he meant he would never leave. Maybe it was just exhaustion and my drug-addled brain misfiring. Maybe I was insecure. But when Bill didn't show up Saturday morning, I got mad at him. I expected him to be with me. I needed him and felt weak and vulnerable. I began to think that maybe he was only with me out of pity. I was hurt, and when he returned from his R&R on Monday, I broke things off.

"Here I am, at the lowest point in my life, and you just left me," I told him, getting short of breath. "Go away! I don't want anything to do with you. I need to think things through, and I have to do that alone."

He tried to protest—to tell me he loved me. He tried to get me to listen. But no amount of pleading would have done him any good. I had made up my mind. "I don't need your pity! And don't bother calling me. I don't want to talk to you."

The following week, Dr. Suh removed the catheters and stitches, cleaned my wounds and replaced my giant bandages. But the pain was still there, made worse by the self-inflicted beating I had just given my heart. When I got home, I crawled up to my room, where I confined myself to bed for five more weeks—taking pain killers, worrying about who would take care of my kids and feeling sorry for myself.

The physical process of healing took several months, and I was bedridden for the first six weeks while surface incisions closed up and muscle and other deep tissues regenerated. Drs. Kodama and Suh had recommended physical therapy, but I never started it. I didn't have anyone available to regularly drive me to appointments, not to mention the pain caused by even sitting up in bed or turning my body was unbearable. Instead I tried to do some of the prescribed exercises at home. Gradual stretching was about all I could handle. Mainly I lay in bed—meditating and praying to heal my heart, mind and soul, as well as my body.

After the wounds from the first surgery scarred over, I went through another series of surgeries to reinforce tissue grafts and fully reshape and rebuild the new breast, which included a service I was not expecting: a new nipple, complete with an areola tattoo. With no nerve endings to allow for sensation, the nipple was purely for the purpose of symmetry, which I found interesting, considering my belly button had been permanently stretched two inches to the left.

My half-sister gave me a CD called *Music of the Angels* as a gift during my long recovery, and I set my portable stereo to play it continuously in my room. The soothing music helped quiet my thoughts and allowed me to open my mind so that I could honestly confront my demons. As I began to reflect on the previous twenty-five years, the same question kept insinuating itself: What is most important? Reviewing all the decisions I had made, both good and bad, I always came back to this question. I figured that until I had the answer, I could not make a plan for the direction I wanted my life to go next.

If, God willing, I survived cancer and still had some time left on earth, I had to make sure it was time well spent. I had worked to simplify my life externally—like solving my financial problems. Now I vowed to simplify things so I could heal internally.

With the time I had left, I would focus only on the things that really mattered and made a positive impact on me, my family and other people who needed my help. I tried to discard everything else—petty grievances, negative feelings, prejudice, material wants, vanity, etc. I would accept the limitations of others, as well as my own. Doing this would enable me to see myself and my relationships more clearly—and to love myself so that I could more fully love and be loved by others. In meditation I tried to unload all these impurities of my spirit and allowed them to be carried off on the wings of angels.

Before my surgery, I never had the luxury of time to methodically chart a course for my life. I had simply reacted and adapted as best I could. I went from one life event, financial crisis, relationship and job to another, often feeling as though I were losing rather than gaining something and struggling to achieve balance between work and family. With my focus divided, I could not give the important things in my life the attention they deserved. It did not take weeks to figure out who and what those were: my family, Devotion to Children and Bill. I also tried to think about how all my life, I had been looking for true love. But what is love? I asked myself.

That puzzle would require much more thought.

The more I considered the question, the more I realized that true love was exactly what Bill had demonstrated to me ever since we'd met. It had taken me a lifetime to recognize that true love is first learning how to love, respect and be honest with yourself. Only then can you truly and genuinely begin to love, respect and be honest with someone else without expectations, conditions or reservations.

Bill had been completely honest with me in every way. He had generously given me his time, compassion, understanding and resources. And he had asked for nothing in return but mutual respect. He was a man of integrity. He was, quite simply, a good man. I owed him an apology and my sincere wish for his future happiness—whether or not things worked out between the two of us.

I told myself that as soon as I gained enough strength to get out of bed on my own and walk with my torso pointed vertically, I would call him.

Starting to feel more like myself again and having sorted through a lifetime of feelings during my long days and nights alone, it was time to express them to Bill. As I listened to the phone ring, a flood of disorganized thoughts began to crystallize. All my life I had been looking for the joy of true, lasting love—for a man who truly loved me. I thought I had found that first with Binh and then with Chuong, but I was wrong. Then I thought I had found it with Bill, but that had not worked out the way I expected. Yes, I had been through a horrible ordeal and endured weeks of excruciating pain. But that was no excuse for the way I had turned Bill away and cut off all communications.

I broke up with him, I reminded myself. *So if he's found someone else, maybe we can still be friends. I love him. I cannot be selfish. No matter who he's with, he deserves happiness after everything he has done for me.*

I didn't expect much in response from Bill, but I needed him to know that I still appreciated him. I was not sure if he would hang up once he recognized my voice. I just hoped I would be able to get all my thoughts out quickly and clearly.

Thankfully, he was polite enough to listen quietly as I wound my way through my rationalization for what happened between us a few weeks before. It was an apology and hopeful philosophy mixed in equal parts.

"I've had the chance to do a lot of thinking since the day you left," I told him. "I know that you're a good man. A caring man. And I truly love you for it. You deserve more than what I was able to give. Wherever you and I go from here, I want the best for you. I want you to be happy."

I could hear nothing on his end but sensed he might be growing impatient. So I continued, "You've been a good friend to me. I could not have gotten through surgery without you. I want to thank you, and I hope we can still be friends."

"Rosemary," he said at last, "I don't want to be friends." I braced myself, thinking, I guess I deserve what's next.

"I don't want to be just your friend. I can't," he stated. "When you wouldn't listen to me—when you wouldn't call me and told me not to call you—that hurt. I knew you were mad, but I couldn't let that stop me. I called your kids behind your back almost every day to see how you were doing. I love you, and I will always love you."

The Christian faith teaches that there is glory after suffering. At last I felt I understood this wisdom completely. Because after enduring so much pain, I had finally found my true love and my path. My heart sang with joy.

By summer, not long after Bill and I reconciled, I began to reassert some control in our relationship. I made it clear to Bill that if we were going to date, it would be for a purpose, not just for fun.

"I date to eventually get married," I told him, sticking to my principles. "I have to know this is going somewhere."

It may seem that I was being too demanding so soon after we got back together. But this didn't come from out of the blue. Early in our relationship, Bill told me he would never get married again. He had gone through two previous divorces and was not looking forward to a potential third. This was one reason we had been platonic friends for so long before getting serious. But now the game had changed, and I wanted him to know the rules had changed too. Dating without a purpose was a deal-breaker for me.

I assured him I was not rushing us to the altar and that I would not pressure him, but that I wanted us to at least be heading in that direction. Bill agreed.

I had another important decision to make. Given my slow recovery and the certainty that my health would be an ongoing concern, I knew my days of working seven days a week were over. Being a stylist had been my life for twenty years, and the bustling salon was my world. As financially rewarding as that life could be, it required too much time and energy, and my body would not hold up to it anymore.

In fact, deep down I believed the rigorous grind and stress of managing Beauty and Bliss may have contributed to my health issues. When I sold the business, I thought the new owner would manage it in a way that would allow me to concentrate on what I most loved doing—making people beautiful. Instead, his erratic behavior just added to my usual work stress. As soon as I handed over the salon at the end of 2000, the new owner began systematically destroying everything I had built since its grand opening. He mistreated employees and customers alike. He fired many of my experienced staff members and replaced them with novices. He was, at times, both physically and verbally abusive. The day he threw a brush at me, I walked out to rejoin my old boss at Master Touch.

Just when I thought I had left the insanity of Beauty and Bliss behind me, the new owner would not pay me the $75,000 he owed for the sale of the salon. He also failed to pay rent for ten months, which accounted for another $100,000 he would never pay me. He eventually sold all of the salon's contents in a yard sale. My name was still on the three-year lease, and now the landlord was coming after me for $360,000! I learned about all of this just after my surgery, and the horrible situation dragged on throughout my long recovery.

The landlord sued me. I went to court hoping to resolve the issue but lost the case because my lawyer was not able to prepare me in time. I considered filing bankruptcy or selling my house to pay the landlord. After all I had done to climb out of the financial abyss, I was getting pulled down again. I called Bill, my greatest calming influence, for advice. He advised me to sell the house and then helped me find a new lawyer to successfully reduce my penalty and help me avoid bankruptcy.

I was now forced to consider another new career. I was starting over, which was not as daunting a thought as it had been in the past. Having succeeded in rebooting my life a few times before, I was more confident about looking for a new career. I also had Bill, who recommended I consider real estate.

Real estate was by no means an easy career, but it would offer me some key benefits, not the least of which was a more flexible schedule. After working most every weekend for decades, this was a big deal for me. More importantly, the job would not be as physically demanding as my salon work, which often required standing for eight to ten hours at a time. Of course, Bill's suggestion was not completely selfless. Working in the same industry would allow us to see each other more often. Finally, a real estate career would allow me more freedom and provide more opportunities to meet new people, which could only help Devotion to Children. I agreed it was worth a try.

I was happy to learn that obtaining a real estate license required absolutely no shorthand skills. Bill's help was invaluable during the six weeks I studied for the exam. And by late 2001, I was a certified, real estate agent with Long & Foster.

After twenty years of owning my own business and having survived the lawsuit over the Beauty and Bliss lease, I chose commercial real estate. I wanted to help other small-business owners succeed, while avoiding some of the pitfalls I had discovered along the way.

Bill's proposal came in the summer of 2002, after months of casual window shopping for (and then stalking of) an antique sapphire ring from a jeweler in Lewes, Delaware. I had seen it the first time he took me there with him, and it was love at first sight. Whenever he returned from a beach trip, I would ask, "Is the ring still there?"

He would give me a reassuring, "Yep, still there."

Playfully prodding him, I would add, "If we don't get it soon, someone else will!"

One weekend on his way home from a solo trip to the coast, Bill called and asked me out for dinner. I told him my daughter-in-law and granddaughter were coming over, and we were ordering Chinese food. I promised to bring him some leftovers as a consolation.

The visit with my daughter-in-law and the baby ended later than expected. By the time I got to Bill's house, he was fast asleep, tired from two days in the sun and a grueling drive home in heavy traffic. I hated to wake him but knew he probably had not eaten.

I went to the kitchen to heat up a plate of food while Bill slowly came back to life. When he finally appeared—T-shirt rumpled, gym shorts too short and blond hair standing straight up—he grumbled, "I have bad news. They sold your ring."

"What?!" My mood took a nosedive. For a second I wanted to let him get his own dinner. "I told you!" I said.

He paused as my reaction downgraded from full-blown hurricane to mere tropical depression, then said, "But ... I also have some good news."

"Really, what?" I asked, thinking to myself, This had better be very good news, because I'm devastated right now!

"The blond top bought it!" he said with a devious grin, referring to my nickname for him. "It's in your purse."

I ran to find my purse and began rummaging through it. "I can't find it," I claimed. "You're not telling me the truth."

He reached into the purse and pulled out a black velvet box. I thrust my hand towards him in anticipation. As he opened the box, my limbs tingled. There it was—the blue sapphire glimmering in an antique platinum setting with diamonds. It was perfect.

Just before I extended my finger, Bill blurted, "Will you marry me?"

"Absolutely!" I said, unable to contain my excitement. Then we were both laughing. "But wait a minute. This was not very romantic," I joked. "No candles, no music, no fancy dinner. And look at you. You look like you just crawled out of bed. Your hair is really standing up on end. And you didn't even kneel down to propose."

"Girl, you didn't give me the chance to do all that!" he said with a heavy sigh.

My dinner with my daughter-in-law had apparently foiled his proposal plans. But we had both learned by then that things don't always go as expected. Real life does not follow a storybook script. While presentation was important, what really mattered were results. As quirky as the proposal was, we were both extremely happy with the outcome that night.

Now we had a wedding to plan.

In the Vietnamese culture, grooms are solely responsible for funding weddings. Not so in American culture, as I had learned from my dear salon clients. Luckily, after selling the townhouse and paying legal fees to fight the lawsuit filed by the landlord of Beauty and Bliss, I still had a little money left over. I was determined to embark on my final voyage into holy matrimony as an equal.

I started planning our celebration right away, knowing I would have to trim costs here and there. It would be simple, yet tasteful. To achieve this balance, Bill and I put our resourceful heads together. Celine Mai—a good friend who worked with me at Beauty by Thai and who was extremely talented with crocheting—made my dress. I bought my own flowers from an inexpensive florist. We stocked the bar ourselves and arranged a good deal with a caterer with whom Bill had previously worked. But with a guest list of more than 200 people, renting a reasonably priced reception hall was a more difficult task. Most venues were asking for several thousand dollars just to rent the space. My favorite was Meadowlark Botanical Gardens in Vienna, Virginia. With its sprawling gardens, walkways lined with early fall colors and wedding gazebo on the water, it reminded me of my childhood, watching in wonder as my father contentedly tended his own gardens. Its $8,000 price tag, however, was beyond my budget.

Then Bill got really creative. He was already in negotiations to buy the building that once housed the old Reston Visitors' Center, intending to turn the empty, 3,000-square-foot property overlooking a small, manmade lake into the new headquarters for his real estate development business. Bill was very active in the early development of Reston, which gave the property sentimental value for him. And the wide-open interior space, artful landscaping and serene views made it the perfect alternative to Meadowlark. So although Bill had not yet finalized the deal, he asked the property owner if we could borrow it for the wedding. The owner generously agreed, and we got our picturesque ceremony on the water at no extra charge.

We married at noon on September 22, 2002. Bang walked me down the aisle, and as I stood in front of my friends and family, holding hands with Bill, everything finally felt exactly as it should. I was enrobed in natural beauty and love. Butterflies danced across a brilliant patchwork of chrysanthemums. In the early fall whisper of rustling leaves and sway of tall grasses, I could hear my father's approval. I had found an everlasting happiness, and I imagined he had found a small measure of peace knowing I would walk side-by-side out of that botanical garden with someone who loved me unconditionally.

Even the most beautiful, poetic wedding story has its flaws. After the perfect ceremony and reception, Bill and I hit a major bump in the road to wedded bliss. The week we returned home from our honeymoon, Bill's secretary called with bad news. Our minister had not been licensed to perform weddings in Virginia.

Apparently, the minister had moved back into the area from out of state and had not yet gotten the proper license. I freaked out. We had our big day, signed a marriage license, moved in together and went on our honeymoon. Now they were saying we weren't married!

When the shock wore off, we figured there was an easy fix. We would take off work the next day, go to the courthouse and sign something to clear up the whole mess. It turned out to be much more difficult than we expected. At the courthouse, a clerk behind a glass partition told us we would need to have a lawyer petition the court and get a judge to rule the marriage legitimate. This would take time. Ours was only the second case of its kind in the entire state.

Three months later, our lawyer got us in front of a judge, who pronounced us, legitimately and at long last, husband and wife. It was the third and last marriage for both of us.

I held on to my part-time job at Master Touch as I continued to ease into the real estate business ... and my marriage. I felt the need to help pay for my healthcare, to demonstrate that my relationship with my new husband was grounded in love and mutual respect, not financial need. In fact, until the day before the wedding, when I signed a pre-nuptial agreement, I knew absolutely nothing about Bill's wealth. From what I could see, as a dedicated bachelor, he lived a relatively modest existence.

After closing my first two real estate deals—I sold a drycleaner's and a church—I felt confident enough to quit the beauty industry for good. When I decided to become a commercial real estate agent, I didn't know that less than ten percent of commercial agents are women. A woman agent with slanted eyes, a flat nose and brown hair, who speaks broken English, is even rarer.

But always one to be resourceful, I quickly turned my liabilities into assets. Being the shortest in the group, wearing a healthy application of makeup and using an authoritative voice makes me memorable. With my experiences at Beauty and Bliss I developed a genuine care for my clients. And my service to others has helped me stand out in my profession. These things have helped me create an indelible, if accidental, brand as an agent, and I've been a top producer with Long & Foster since 2002. With good earning potential and more exposure to corporate principals, Devotion to Children has a greater opportunity to raise awareness while gaining sponsorships. I've never looked back, and Devotion to Children has continued to grow.

※

We held Devotion's inaugural Red, Heart and Soul Gala a year later in November 2003—four years after Bill and I met and four years after I suggested to the Devotion Board of Directors that we tap into his fundraising expertise.

As was the tradition for Devotion fundraisers at the time, Red, Heart and Soul served a dual purpose. It was also a housewarming party for the new home Bill and I purchased so that we would have more room for hosting family, guests and fundraising events.

We raised about $3,000 for Devotion that night. And though the event cost more than that to put on, we had taken a giant leap forward in fundraising. We had launched our signature fall event, which would kick off the holiday season of giving for years to come.

In the past few years, Bill and Bang have taken on leadership roles with the organization as advisory board members, overseeing an amazing period of expansion. Together with Devotion's Board of Directors and other advisory board members, they infused the mission with a new level of passion, focus and sophisticated coordination— both internally and with other organizations. To address the persistent, growing childcare challenges families were facing in our area, Devotion needed to not only raise money but also develop more partnerships with other like-minded people and nonprofits.

With a steady increase in our fundraising and number of partnerships, we were able to extend the reach of our vision. We also began to tackle larger social issues affecting many families' ability to become self-sufficient. From our original goal—to provide quality child-care assistance so parents of children under age six could hold jobs outside the home—Devotion's reach grew to include tuition assistance, early childhood education programs and other advocacy for families with young children. These were all challenging issues I could relate to as a single mom.

For many years, Devotion to Children has been inching forward, our volunteer board and event staff doing what we can, when we can, and with little more than our mission statement to guide our efforts. Now it has moved upward with the help of the angels on our dedicated board of directors, advisory board and growing group of volunteers.

In 2010 Devotion to Children added a second major fundraiser to its calendar—the first annual Mother's Day Four-Mile Run. The same year, proceeds from the Red, Heart and Soul Fall Gala reached our $100,000 milestone for the first time. And in 2011 we held our first annual Cards 4 Kids Texas Hold 'Em Tournament.

With all our events in 2012, Devotion to Children was able to raise more than $150,000 to help working families. We funded the participation of more than 400 children in early childhood programs and other services provided by our five partners. For my work with our organization, the Association of Fundraising Professionals honored me in 2010 as the recipient of the Outstanding Fundraising Volunteer Award. In 2012, I was also presented with the Asian Leader Award by the Connected International Meeting Professionals Association. More important than the personal recognition, I was humbled by the opportunity to continue raising Devotion's cause to a national level.

In the past year, we've made great strides, but we're not stopping there. In order for Devotion to Children to make the greatest possible impact and progress towards ending the cycle of poverty for families in this country, the organization needs to grow in its political influence. We need a louder voice to help raise awareness of the critical need for affordable, quality childcare in America and beyond.

It started with my solo voice—the voice of an overwhelmed but passionate bumblebee. And over the decades, countless real-life angels have added their voices to my chorus. Now I'm working to recruit even more selfless singers for our choir. Telling you my story has just been the first step.

Chapter 14: *Transformed and Ascending*

It began with one emotion (love). I love children. Then came a vision. Children—children everywhere. Children who grow up being productive, happy, free. Then I had an idea. I see unwanted children, and it breaks my heart. I see fearful mothers who don't know what to do with their kids, feeling trapped and then hating the kids. Some even kill their kids.

So I have a solution—the house of Devotion to Children in Poverty. It's at my house, and I am the house mother. We take care of kids. Whoever doesn't want their kids but happens to have them, bring them to me. Someday, if you want them back, you are welcome to have them, but I'll take care of your kids because I love them and I love you, too.

You can make money and donate that to me to raise your kids, or you don't have to give me anything. I do it because I want to do it. Maybe the government will help me. Maybe people who love kids will help me.

– Reflections recorded in my personal journal, 1997

As a survivor I fight a battle every day. And every day the love for my family and passion for Devotion to Children's cause helps me to overcome whatever stands in my way.

In January 2007, during a routine checkup with my gynecologist, I received some concerning test results: I had a tumor in my uterus. Whether it was malignant or benign, my doctor did not want to take any chances, and he ordered a radical hysterectomy.

In August of that year, a mammogram showed another lump— now on my left breast. This time my doctor ordered a lumpectomy and radiation. I skipped the radiation, opting instead to take a drug called Tamoxifen. I had been prescribed Tamoxifen after my first round of cancer but soon stopped taking it. I quickly realized that it had one particularly nasty side effect: it made me extremely depressed.

Cooped up in my room, unable to move for hours on end and for several weeks during my recovery, I experienced such intense feelings of dread and sorrow that I told my doctors, "I may have survived the TRAM flap, but now I might die of depression." As soon as I stopped taking the drug, my energy came back, and the sadness melted away.

After this, my third surgery (and second one related to cancer), there was no choice. I had to take the drug. I have been taking it—and fending off those meddling feelings of melancholy—ever since.

The best way I have found to help avoid deep depression is to keep busy, almost obsessively busy. But not doing just anything. I have to do something meaningful for me and for other people. If I slow down, the sadness creeps back in and steals my power and motivation. Some days I have a hard time getting out of bed. But if I can stay focused and continue driving myself forward, then I know my day will be okay.

The momentum of my cause and love for my family carries me through, leaving me no time for the sadness, self-pity or negativity that can cause a person to give up.

Now I have two enemies at the gate: cancer, which may come back, and depression, which is ever present with each daily dose of the drug I must take. Those are the facts. I can choose to do one of three things going forward. I can deny the facts, fear them or transform them. I have chosen the third option. With the time I have left, however long that may be, I will devote myself to my life's mission of raising awareness of the need for affordable, quality childcare. Instead of focusing inward, wondering what's going to happen to me, I live for every moment. And I look for ways to help others and build a legacy—one strong enough to make a bigger difference long after I'm gone.

For now I stay busy—focused on this goal that helps me manage my depression and thoughts about the cancer. When I am productive and do things for the right reasons, with good intentions and a purpose, I am able to see through the darkness—like when I immerse myself in fundraising events for Devotion. Focusing on something much greater than myself fills me with the energy I need to push myself. Without that sense of purpose and urgency in my life, I might have given up like those women—and young girls—who paraded past La Cave Academy day after lonely day.

There have been times during my American experience when I would have liked nothing better than to lie down, pull a quilt over my head and say, "I don't care." It's frightening how strong that urge can become, how easy it seems.

But I do care. So I have to tell myself, If you just lie down and cry, what's the point? Who are you helping then? Instead, I choose (no, I dare) to care—so that I can keep going. Every day in everything I do, I try my best to help make the world a better place, and I want to encourage every person I know and meet to do the same. In this same spirit, I invite those who have read my story to consider joining me in support of Devotion to Children's mission.

Epilogue: *A Legacy ... for Other People's Children*

Surviving cancer made me stronger in many ways. It changed me—improved me, I believe. It changed the way I look at people and the world. It changed my values and helped me understand the true meaning of love, integrity and personal relationships. My diagnosis and treatment was, in a way, very liberating. It helped me realize how fragile life is and that I can only change things within my control. Today I see people in a gentler way. I try to banish judgment and appreciate everyone, regardless of their backgrounds or circumstances.

I live for every moment and want to do as much as I can with the time I have left. It's not about the quantity of time; it's about the quality of what I do with that time. I want a meaningful life and a meaningful death—and to leave a legacy that will benefit and empower the next generation (and the next). I wish everyone could approach life this way—whether they struggle with cancer, financial troubles, an addiction or any of life's other hardships.

Whenever I think of the orphans I met in Da Lat, my heart breaks. I was not able to help any of them. Now, any chance I get to make life easier for even one child, to help him or her feel loved and important, I take it. They may not be my children, but I love them all as my own. Devotion to Children's very existence is based on this fundamental concept.

You may ask, What about your own kids? Didn't they need their mother and father? Of course. But I don't think they needed to be coddled. The fact they have all graduated from college and gone on to become productive members of society and successful at whatever they have put their minds and hearts to is, in my opinion, the best evidence of that.

When my kids were sick, I was there for them. And whenever I could, I brought them to the salon and spent time with them there. But what my kids needed most was a roof over their heads and food in their bellies. To provide the necessities, I had to work at whatever job I could find. If that meant working eighteen hours a day and seeing them only in the mornings and sometimes at night, or sometimes not at all, so be it. That was the sacrifice I had to make, and I often felt guilty about it. But my children, like me, were able to adapt. In the time I could spend with them, I think I was able to instill values and show, by my example, the strength they needed to succeed. They grew up knowing how to take care of themselves.

When I was getting Bang and Mai out of Vietnam, I was their protector and a survivor. When we arrived in America, I was still in survival mode, but my focus shifted in light of our situation, suppressing one instinctual need (being a nurturing mother) to ensure my success in fulfilling another (being a provider). I did my best to let my kids know I loved them and that I would still keep them safe but, as much as it pained me at times, I could not shower them with the attention they probably deserved. I was not able to spend as much time with them as they (and I) might have wished. I have no doubt there were many times they quietly resented me for it.

I completely understand those feelings. But what my children may not realize is how much I actually do know about them even though I could not always be there. I feel for the responsibility Ann had to take on, being the oldest. Karen was always a great student and tried to avoid conflict whenever possible. Bang, my only son, had to deal with the traditional expectations of an Asian family. Mai, so beautiful and rebellious, managed to handle the difficult balancing act of moving back and forth between two different cultures. After dealing with so much at a young age, Anh learned to cope by not letting little things distract her. Elizabeth was always sweet and funny in her own way as a child. Kim is very intelligent and empathetic. She cares a lot about others, sometimes maybe too much. She is still uncertain about which direction her life will take her, but I trust she will do well, because her heart is always in the right place.

I have always cared very much about my whole family, but my communication with my children was not always good when they were growing up. I have, therefore, had to rationalize those earlier years of struggle and separation by telling myself that the sacrifices I made for my children's sake helped them become the strong, successful and self-sufficient adults they are today. I know I was not a perfect parent. None of us are. But I hope my kids understand now that I did everything in my power to give them what they needed while making sure they had the best available care. Even though I could not be with them all the time, they were always on my mind and close to my heart. I still have much to make up for.

In November 2005, my son delivered the opening remarks for Devotion's Red, Heart and Soul Gala. That night Bang helped ease some of the guilt still weighing on me. By the end of his heartfelt introduction, my mascara was running. This sentiment of his was particularly gratifying:

> *Though there's very little I recall from my early childhood, what I do remember is that there was always someone to care for me and my sister when my mother wasn't around. It wasn't the same as spending time with her, but I knew she was working hard on our behalf, and I took comfort in the fact that someone was looking after us.*

Each year during the Red, Heart and Soul Gala, I take time to reflect on how my life, as well as the lives of those people helped by Devotion, would be different had I not gotten out of Vietnam when I did—the way I did.

It is tempting to ask "what if?" What if I had become a nun as a young lady or taken the "safer" route? Would my life have been as rewarding?

These questions always lead me to conclude that had I made different decisions, I would not have the same family and friends I cherish today.

My grandmother wanted for me to have a quiet, safe life, but I don't think that would have been nearly as satisfying. I have, of course, experienced my share of misfortune while leading this life I've chosen. Still, my family's struggles pale in comparison to those of the millions of children who are unable to help themselves and suffer in poverty today. I firmly believe what we do for ourselves in this life doesn't matter nearly as much as what we do for others.

Twenty-five years ago, my client Kevin McGuire first told me I should write a book. A few people even volunteered to write it for me. When I first heard the suggestion, I laughed. *Who would want to hear about my life?* I thought. *What have I done that's so special?* The idea came up again not long before I married Bill. Things were going well, more or less, with Beauty and Bliss, and Devotion was just starting to make an impact. I began to take the book idea more seriously, thinking it could be another good way to shine a light on the importance of affordable, quality childcare—and maybe even raise some money for Devotion in the process. I mentioned it to Bang when he left Morgan Stanley and moved back to Virginia to work with Bill in real estate.

"Why, Mom?" he asked. "You won't have anything really good to say until I'm successful. When that happens, then you can write your book." He may have been half-joking, but there was a lot of truth in what he said. My success can be measured only by how successful, productive and compassionate my children are as members of society.

Bang worked with Bill for a few years before Morgan Stanley persuaded him to come back. He is currently responsible for the company's investment banking business in Vietnam and the Philippines. He now lives in Vietnam with his wife and children while working and traveling extensively in Asia. Even as busy as his life has become, my son remains close to me and stays involved with Devotion to Children.

Mai, who at just six months old clung to life and me on our journey from Saigon to Washington, D.C., is now married and has three children of her own. She graduated from Mary Washington College and runs her own health-care consulting company called Mai Health Now, while she also pursues a Master of Science in Global Health Sciences from George Mason University.

Anh graduated from the College of William and Mary and holds a marketing position with the prestigious architectural firm Little Diversified Architectural Consulting. While pursuing a Master of Architecture degree from Virginia Tech, Anh has already established a successful career helping her company win many high-profile contracts, including one with Donald Trump. She married in 2011.

Elizabeth and Kim both graduated from the University of Virginia and work for the global consulting firm, The Advisory Board Company. Elizabeth has recently married in 2013.

My girls, like their brother, support Devotion as much as they can. Their volunteer efforts have helped Devotion achieve more than it ever could have without them. They remain vital to its continued success.

My stepdaughters also are doing very well. Ann is married with three children and has a successful career with the cosmetics company, Trish McEvoy. Karen graduated from the University of Virginia and works as an accountant. She also has three children of her own.

Bill's children, Kim and Andy, both work with him at Tetra Partnership. Kim, a single mom, has a son. Andy is married with two children.

For years I have worked and prayed for my children's success and could not be more proud of them. They are the true heart of my success story—one that has always been about them, not me. Along with Bill, the love of my life and my faithful partner, our family stands arm-in-arm, facing the world. They give me reasons "why" every day— just by being who they are, despite hardships and having a mother who was often unable to be there for them as she worked to brighten their futures. I know that "life is a journey and not a destination," so I am sure that my children will have their own share of challenges. I hope and pray that through my personal experiences and example, my children will have the strength to overcome their own life difficulties when and if they present themselves.

It is because of what my kids have achieved that I was finally able to write this book. I would like to declare that this story has a happily-ever-after ending. But our story goes on. It must go on so that Devotion to Children—my other purpose in life—can continue to grow and help children and families around the globe.

Chuong died unexpectedly in October 2010 on a trip to the U.S. His passing gave me another opportunity to contemplate life and the nature of love. He never apologized for what he had done to our family. I have since found peace with that. I found my closure when I realized that the demise of our relationship was not my fault. It was his way of stepping aside in order to let me flourish.

I know Chuong loved us. And I loved him once. I can still see the person he was before he left his family and tried to regain his status—and maybe his identity—in Vietnam. In pictures of him, I see a loving father who gave his family many happy memories. I know how proud he was of his children.

This is the way I want to remember him.

Chuong's death reinforced my understanding of true love and what it takes to find and sustain it. When I married Bill, I was finally able to put my finger on its definition.

I had loved both of my previous husbands. I would not have married either without it. But those were different kinds of love. With Binh it was youthful naïveté and romantic idealism. With Chuong it was about realistic pragmatism and shared circumstances. These led me to what I thought was true love.

But after ten years with Bill, I believe that for true love to last, we must first know and be comfortable with ourselves. We must love ourselves, because we must have something before we can give it away to others. And the more you give, the more you'll get in return. In that way, giving and receiving are the same thing. This is true for money, respect and love.

Bill has always told me that for love to last between two people in a relationship, the effort has to be greater than fifty-fifty; it has to be more like eight-eighty. We have both done our best to practice this concept every day. I am thankful that with Bill I found what I was looking for at last. I have my true love and my best friend.

> *From a distance, everyone's life looks like a painting—some may be considered beautiful works of art, some ugly and misunderstood to the untrained eye. But when you move in closer to see all the individual brush strokes and flaws, you realize the imperfections—the challenges— are part of what makes life more interesting. Our ability to embrace and see beyond the imperfections is what gives us our character. It's what makes life beautiful.*

– Another personal journal entry, undated

Throughout my life, with faith in God's plan, help from my many angels without wings and a devotion to all children, especially my own, I have transformed tragedy into something truly meaningful for my family.

I've gone to hell and back—experienced war, poverty, homelessness, painful relationships and sickness. I can share my experiences and help others navigate the treacherous waters because I've been there and know how difficult it is. Everybody has challenges, but how do we perceive and respond to those challenges?

If you, dear reader, remember nothing else I have shared with you in these pages, please remember this: Everything happens for a reason, and you will get through it. You are always stronger than you may think.

I don't have a Ph.D. and I am not a psychologist. But as I have often stated, there are many ways to learn. In addition to my work in real estate and with Devotion to Children, I've recently taken on a new challenge. By using my life experience as a way to help others who are facing difficult times, I have transformed myself into a life coach. Yes, ever the busy bumblebee, I'm back to working three jobs—still defying gravity. I am able to offer practical insights to my clients. I can tell them there is light at the end of the tunnel, because I have been in the tunnel myself, faced my demons there and emerged stronger than before. This, I think, is what gives me a unique perspective and knowledge to share with my clients. I can tell them there is a way out of the darkness, because I have had to find it—more than once.

I never became a nun or a secretary, and I have not started an orphanage. But with the timely help of a diverse group of beggars and angels, I believe I've made a difference. I envision a time—maybe not during my lifetime but someday—when U.S. lawmakers will consider affordable, quality childcare to be as critical to our children's futures as higher education, universal healthcare or homeland security. With the heroic efforts of Devotion's all-volunteer staff, whom I can never thank enough, I am confident our mission to achieve and sustain universal childcare will carry on long after I've departed.

Dear Mom,

Inside these pages, you will find a wonderful story about life and achieving your childhood dreams. I hope it will serve to inspire you as you write your own story to share with the world. Thank you for your ongoing love, support, and guidance. I'm very proud to be your son and feel incredibly blessed to be able to call you mom. Happy Mother's Day.

Your loving son, Bang

– Inscription inside a gifted copy of *The Last Lecture* by Randy Pausch, May 11, 2008

Dr. Annette Ficker—the pediatrician who took such good care of Mai when we first arrived in D.C.—died July 31, 2009. I did not know about her passing until more than two years later, after I began writing this book. I had not seen or spoken to her since the day I took Mai home from Children's Hospital. But in just a few days, she profoundly touched my life and gave me another reason to believe in the inherent goodness of most people.

After reading her obituary in *The Washington Post*, I discovered how much the two of us actually had in common—as mothers, nomads and women of faith who devoted their lives to the care of children, whether or not they were our own. Cancer and divorce are other circumstances we would share, although those unfortunate commonalities would not develop for either of us until long after our brief acquaintance ended.

Here is an excerpt from the *Post's* obituary, which ran on August 11, 2009, for "Frances Annette Ficker, pediatrician":

> *Frances Annette Ficker, 70, a pediatrician in the Washington area for more than 40 years, died of cancer July 31, 2009 ... While in medical school at St. Louis University School of Medicine, she served a six-month fellowship in India in 1968. In 1970, she joined Children's National Medical Center, where she served for more than 25 years. She also worked at the Hospital for Sick Children and the Greater Baden Medical Clinic in Upper Marlboro ... She was born Frances Annette Heiser in Tryon, N.C. Because her father was an Army officer, she lived in several places while growing up ... Dr. Ficker was an active member of Our Lady of Mercy Catholic Church in Potomac, where she sang in the choir and served as a Eucharistic minister. She and her family went to the summer Olympics in Los Angeles, Seoul and Barcelona. She also accompanied her daughter to triathlon races throughout the United States, including Hawaii ... She was an avid gardener and enjoyed baking peach pies using peaches from her son's fruit and vegetable stand. Her marriage to Robin Ficker ended in divorce. Survivors include three children ... a brother and a sister.*

Learning of her death—and catching a glimpse of who she was in life from this news clipping—prompted me to think more about how we, as human beings, no matter our individual ethnic, social or theological backgrounds, are all connected in our ongoing search for meaning, love and acceptance. From this attempt to summarize an amazing life, it appears Dr. Ficker remained close to her children until the end and was able to spend her final years in the company of her loving family.

My knowledge of her life may be limited to this snapshot and my brief encounter with her in 1975, but I sincerely hope this is true.

✺

Devotion to Children is the first step towards my ultimate goal of achieving universal childcare in the U.S. and an ideal future for families everywhere trying to raise educated, healthy, thoughtful children. I believe there is a desperate need worldwide for a shift in the way childcare and education are (or are not) made available to working families. In 2012 there were more than 21 million children under age five in the U.S., according to Child Care Aware of America. Nearly 11 million of them (fifty-two percent) were in some type of child-care arrangement every week. Of those, 3.2 million (twenty-eight percent) lived with single, working moms and 1.6 million (fourteen percent) lived below the poverty level.

Education will always be one of the leading predictors of success. Certainly there are many ways to learn and many ways to obtain an education. I'm living proof of that. But research shows that children who participate in high-quality childcare and pre-school programs are more likely to enter kindergarten with the knowledge and skills they need to be successful in school for years to come. Children who participate in preschool are more likely to graduate from high school and significantly less likely to need welfare or to be involved in criminal activities.

Like having access to public schools or healthcare, I believe every family deserves access to quality and affordable childcare, so that all children can get what they need during the most critical time of their lives. With mothers working outside the home to support their families at the highest rate in history, providing affordable childcare to all families is possibly the best way to disrupt the cycle of poverty. I believe it's time we had a serious discussion about universal childcare. Our society and the world will be better for it.

Would You Like to Help Devotion to Children?

If you have been inspired by my story of survival, optimism, and success, I would be grateful for any support you might offer Devotion to Children. If you would like to make a donation, please visit **www.DevotionToChildren.org** Any amount is worthwhile and will have a positive impact on the lives and futures of deserving children and their working parents. Thank you, and may you be blessed in your own journey.

Acknowledgements

Rosemary Tran Lauer

To my son Bang—I would like to express my loving gratitude for our adventure together and your encouragement to write this book. To my daughters, Anh, Elizabeth and Kim—thanks for your help with Devotion to Children. Your love and support help me to be my best and to continue pursuing my work with Devotion. To my daughter Mai and stepdaughters, Ann and Karen—thanks for putting up with all my imperfections as a mother. And to my husband Bill—thank you for supporting my dreams and for teaching me the meaning of "true love."

My thanks to Mary Marshall and Leslie Gerson for helping my family come to the U.S. from Vietnam.

I would also like to express my deepest gratitude to Scott Beller for his incredible patience, talent and professionalism, to our editor Taylor Mallory Holland for her enthusiasm, generosity, timely support, kindness and integrity, and to Judi Ruttenberg for her timely work with my memoir.

My thanks to my assistants, Karissa Ruano and Mohit Trehan, without whom I would be lost.

My heartfelt gratitude to all those who offered their time, support and guidance for the overall production of Beggars or Angels, particularly Misti Burmeister, Mali Phonpadith, Akia Garnett, Dr. Carol Williams-Nickelson and Dr. Meg Edwards.

I would also like to express my undying gratitude for the many volunteers who have helped Devotion become what it is today. In particular, I would like to recognize Devotion's Board of Directors—including Dr. Beverly Mattson, Dan Ruttenberg, Rick Whealen, Ban Tran,

Sara Zeller, Jahan Jewayni, Yasmine Bonilla and Steve Chiama— as well as our advisory board members—including, Bang Trinh, Bill Lauer, Me-Tin Cheung, Kathleen Kennedy, Germaine Swanson, Lilian Li, Brigitta Toruno, Elizabeth Updike, Akia Garnett, Dr. Carol Williams-Nickelson, Lieu Nguyen, Dr. Ava Nguyen, Jennifer Lee, Grace Lee, Lida Peterson, Drazen Alcocer and Michael Gorman. Also, thank you to past board members—Dr. Emily Woo, Dr. Arlene Heinzman, Dr. Patricia Sanders, Maryanne Datesman, Eric Hovanky, Siu Cheng, Rosa Colello, Joyce Holloway-Wilson and Dr. C.C. Lee (who created Devotion's logo)—and to honorary board member Angie Goff, who has served as Red, Heart and Soul Gala Mistress of Ceremonies since 2008. I would also like to thank Eric Johnson for working with Devotion to create our Legacy Award and Roberto Nickson for producing our Devotion to Children promotional video.

My thanks to Elizabeth Pan, Celine Mai, Tuan Nguyen, Kathy Lipton, Raymond Konan, Emerson Lee, Bob Taylor and all my friends who supported Devotion to Children in its early stages—you are my angels.

Special thanks to the many individual and corporate sponsors who continue to support Devotion's mission, as well as the growing list of Devotion partners—including YMCA, Northern Virginia Family Services, Reston Interfaith, Falls Church-McLean Childcare Center and United Community Ministries—for supporting our cause by providing affordable, quality childcare.

My thanks and love to my mother, father, brothers and sisters. Thank God for you.

Finally, I would like to sincerely thank all the friends who have taught, influenced and inspired me on my journey, as well as the many angels and beggars who helped guide me along the way. If I have failed to thank you, either in person or in these pages, please know that you have truly touched my life, and no act of kindness has gone unnoticed. May God bless you all!

Scott Beller

I met Rosemary in August 2009. We were introduced by Jennifer Sterling, a former high school classmate and friend of mine, with whom I'd recently been reunited thanks to the magic of social media. Jen asked if I'd ever done any ghostwriting, because she had a pro-bono client interested in writing a book about the founding of her nonprofit. Being a savvy freelance writer open to any and all opportunities, of course I said yes. It was not a complete fiction; I'd "ghosted" many bylined articles, Op-Eds and speeches for various clients during my PR career, but this would be my first book.

A few days later, shortly before my youngest daughter Lauren was born, I sat in a small conference room with Rosemary at her real estate office while she shared with me the basic outline of her story. Then she gave me a writing test—not necessarily to determine whether I had the writing chops (she'd already seen some of my best writing samples) but to be sure this six-foot-three Caucasian guy could really empathize with and capture the essence of a not-quite-five-foot-tall Vietnamese woman's rags-to-riches story. Luckily I had something working in my favor: My daughter Morgan. I may not have known what it was like to be a refugee or to start my life over in a foreign country on welfare, but I already knew what it was like to work from home while raising a small child. I knew how critical (and just how difficult) it was to find someone reliable to care for my children while my wife and I worked to help support them.

In November 2009, I attended my first Red, Heart and Soul Gala to meet some members of Rosemary's family and further immerse myself in her world. For the next year, I met with Rosemary as often as our crazy schedules allowed to interview her about every facet of her personal and professional life. Though we began outlining the book in early 2010, the actual writing of the manuscript didn't begin, in earnest, until later that December. As we neared publication, I began to better understand that this was not just my first book; it was my third child. I hope this one has half the potential as my other two.

I first want to thank Rosemary for entrusting me with her story and having faith in my ability to convey it authentically and in a way that would do it justice. And thank you, Jen, for introducing us.

I also want to thank so many others who helped get me here, starting with my family. To my wife Elisabeth—I love you for (among other things) your patience, for taking care of our family so that I might have the freedom to dedicate three long years to developing this manuscript and for only sneaking a peek once ... that I know about. To my amazing daughters, Morgan and Lauren—Thank you for being a constant source of inspiration and laughter, for giving me a greater sense of purpose and for (usually) understanding when Daddy needed quiet time to work. To my mother Mary—thank you for the unconditional love and for always being my greatest (and loudest) cheerleader. To my grandmother Angeral Campbell (aka, "Omi")—your love and generosity got me to and through college in one piece. And to my grandmother Evelyn Beller (aka, "Mamaw"), who celebrated her 100th birthday on February 28, 2013—thank you for instilling in me the love of reading, which in many ways inspired me to become a writer. Your love will continue to inspire me for the rest of my years.

A special thanks to my long-time buddies, Gabriel and EJ, two brothers I met through New Hope Housing's mentoring program when they were just seven and nine years old, respectively (they both tower over me now—talk about humbling!). Gabe's soon to be college-bound, and EJ is already there at Virginia Commonwealth University. Once homeless, these young men (along with Evans, their courageous, single father) gave me my first true understanding of the challenges families struggling to break the cycle of poverty face every day. They also taught me my first lessons about being a responsible parent and about how valuable it is for children to have a father—or father figure—really be there for them. The benefits have certainly been mutual.

I would also like to thank Chino Chapa, my friend and first PR-agency boss, who trusted me enough to give me opportunities to write about important things from day one; Allan Shedlin, my friend, frequent writing collaborator, client, daddying guru, sounding board, role model and reminder that just being a dad isn't enough (it's much more about the doing); Taylor Mallory Holland, my editor, who smoothed out the rough parts (including this sentence!), taking the fruit of my labor and making it that much sweeter; David Christel, prolific ghostwriter, whose early guidance on the ghostwriting craft helped me tackle and shape a lengthy narrative; and Karen Frost, publicist extraordinaire, whose friendship, sage advice, encouragement and referrals have helped me grow my business.

Also, thank you to the long list of friends, family members, colleagues and neighbors who regularly inquired "how's the book coming?" and then politely indulged me as I tried to explain—often at great length and punctuated with heavy sighs. And to Dixon for keeping me (mostly) sane.

About the Authors

Rosemary Tran Lauer is an American success story. When she escaped from war-torn Vietnam in 1975, as a single mother of two young children, she had no college education and spoke little English. Striving for financial independence, she depended on the kindness of friends to help care for her kids while she worked multiple jobs. She relied on welfare benefits to make ends meet when she went back to school. After cosmetology school, she spent more than twenty years in the beauty industry, where she often brainstormed with her salon clients about how to one day help children and families like hers break the cycle of poverty.

In 1994 she founded the nonprofit Devotion to Children to make her vision and the dreams of thousands of needy families a reality. In 2001, after recovering from breast cancer, she earned her commercial real estate license and joined Long & Foster Realty, where she's been a top producer ever since.

Rosemary serves on the Board of Directors for Northern Virginia Family Services (NVFS) and the Board of Advisors for Virginia Commerce Bank, and is active with the Vietnamese Realtor Forum. She's been honored by NVFS's We Are America Now initiative and has received SmartCEO's 2010 Spirited Service Award, the Association of Fundraising Professionals' 2010 Outstanding Fundraising Volunteer Award and The Asian American Chamber of Commerce's 2011 Public Service Award. In 2012 the Connected International Meeting Professional Association presented Rosemary with the Asian Leader Award. The Dulles Regional Chamber of Commerce also recognized Devotion To Children as the 2012 Small Nonprofit of the Year.

Now a philanthropist, business leader, commercial realtor, life coach and happily remarried mother of five, Rosemary lives in Oakton, Virginia, and works tirelessly with her husband Bill to give disadvantaged children and their working parents a brighter future.

Scott Beller is a twenty-year public relations industry veteran, writer, independent consultant and work-at-home dad.

During his PR career, Scott has held leadership positions with some of the world's top agencies—including Fleishman-Hillard, Weber Shandwick and Manning, Selvage & Lee, where he honed his writing skills and developed a number of public information campaigns supporting the improved health, nutrition and quality of life for children and families. His talents have been frequently called upon by some of the most recognized brands—including Nike, SBC Communications Inc., XM Satellite Radio, Dell, Anheuser Busch, Exxon, the American Public University System and NASDAQ.

As a consultant, Scott helped launch DADS Unlimited and REEL FATHERS (www.ReelFathers.com) and is part of Devotion to Children's Advisory Board. He was named 2003 Volunteer of the Year as a youth mentor for New Hope Housing, Northern Virginia's largest provider of shelter, transitional and permanent housing to homeless families. He lives in Arlington, Virginia, with his patient wife Elisabeth and two brilliant, kind, adorable and exhausting daughters.

My Family Then and Now

Me, my brother Dang and my grandmother

A day at the Da Lat market with Bang

Bang holding Mai and her bottle our first year in Washington, D.C., 1976

Me with Bang and Mai on the balcony of our Donnybrook Court apartment, 1977

Beauty by Thai Salon employees (left to right): Trang, Ngoc, me holding my daughter Elizabeth and my daughter Ann

At the 2012 Red, Heart & Soul Fall Gala (left to right): Bang and wife Tina, Elizabeth, me, Bill, Mai and husband Kobus, Kim, Anh and husband Aaron

*Me with Bill—Devotion To Children's 2012
Legacy Award recipient and my true love*

http://dtcpress.com